D1591730

STEP UP with CHINESE

成长

TEXTBOOK 1

编委会

特别顾问：崔希亮
Honorary Consultant　**Xiliang Cui**

顾问：　刘珣　　崔永华
Consultants　**Xun Liu**　**Yonghua Cui**

北京语言大学 Beijing Language & Culture University:

编者：陈丽霞　张兰欣　王枫　徐式婧　黄雯雯
Writers　**Lixia Chen**　**Lanxin Zhang**　**Feng Wang**　**Shijing Xu**　**Wenwen Huang**

美国教育专家 American Educators:

竹露茜　陶洁琳　陈少元　谭大立
Lucy Chu Lee　**Janice Dowd**　**Carol Chen-Lin**　**Dali Tan**

CENGAGE

Australia • Brazil • Mexico • Singapore • United Kingdom • United States

Step Up with Chinese Textbook 1

Senior Regional Director:
Janet Lim

Senior Product Manager:
Lee Hong Tan

Senior Editorial Manager:
Lian Siew Han

Editorial Manager:
Zhao Lan

Senior Development Editor:
Tanmayee Bhatwadekar

Development Editors:
Titus Teo
Kenneth Chow
Wei Yi Ng
Elaine Chew
Willie Ong

Creative Manager:
Melvin Chong

Senior Regional Manager,
Production and Rights:
Pauline Lim

Production Executive:
Rachael Tan

Compositor:
Sok Ling Ong

For product information and technology assistance, contact us at
Cengage Learning Asia Customer Support, 65-6410-1200

For permission to use material from this text or product,
submit all requests online at **cengageasia.com/permissions**
Further permissions questions can be emailed to
asia.permissionrequest@cengage.com

ISBN: 978-981-4246-63-7

Cengage Learning Asia Pte Ltd
151 Lorong Chuan
#02-08 New Tech Park
Singapore 556741

Cengage Learning is a leading provider of customized learning solutions with office locations around the globe, including Singapore, the United Kingdom, Australia, Mexico, Brazil, and Japan. Locate your local office at **cengage.com/global**

Cengage Learning products are represented in Canada by Nelson Education, Ltd.

For information on our Chinese language teaching products, visit **cengagechinese.com**

To learn more about Cengage Learning Solutions, visit **cengageasia.com**

Photo credits:
Getty Images, Thinkstock

Printed in Singapore
Print Number: 05   Print Year: 2017

Welcome to Step Up with Chinese!

Step Up with Chinese is an innovative, standards-based Chinese textbook series for high school students with little or no Chinese background. Highly learner-friendly and task-centered, *Step Up* develops all four language skills while incorporating the principles of ACTFL Five C's – Communication, Cultures, Connections, Comparisons, and Communities. Students will learn all the necessary material to engage others in meaningful communication and gain a better understanding of the Chinese culture.

> "The instructional framework is EXCELLENT! It is nicely aligned with the National Standards." *– Jianhua Bai, Kenyon College*

This series consists of three volumes covering three years of instruction. Each volume includes a Textbook and a Workbook. Each textbook offers ten themed lessons that are structured around key communicative goals. The textbook features a clear, step-by-step approach to help students progress from small "steps" of language usage towards larger communicative goals. Instead of the traditional text-and-vocabulary grammar centered approach, each chapter is broken down into small chunks of patterns to learn and practice. Students will get plenty of practice on new vocabulary and grammar. The activities have been carefully designed so that students develop confidence with the new material before moving to the next step. Each step builds upon previously learned vocabulary and sentence patterns in a systematic way. The integration section at the end of each chapter gives students the opportunity to synthesize and apply what they have learned in more challenging, authentic tasks, further reinforcing their interpretive, interpersonal and presentational skills.

> "I like the way this textbook organizes each chapter. The step-by-step approach makes each task very clear." *– Lihua Li, Berkeley Preparatory School*

The authors have interweaved a variety of cultural content, Chinese culture vis-a-vis Western culture, throughout the program—in the visuals, practice activities, readings, writing activities, cultural snippets and *Fun Time* section of each chapter, to foster students' cultural awareness from a global point of view. The program also reinforces language learning by making connections to students' prior knowledge, their personal experiences and other content areas that are relevant to them.

Step Up with Chinese provides ample support for students to gain a positive learning experience and to become a lifelong learner of Chinese.

> "This is a very up-to-date book that is very appropriate for high school students in the States. The students can really relate to a lot of scenes in the book and see their own lives in the book instead of just knowing someone else's life in China." *– Jie Lei, George C. Marshall High School*

　　《成长》是一套具有开拓性的、专供初学者使用的中学中文教材。本教材的教学理念和目标是根据美国外语教学委员会(ACTFL)的国家语言教学标准(5C)制订的："沟通和交际能力(Communication)"、"文化理解和体验能力(Cultures)"、"与其他学科贯连的能力(Connections)"、"语言、文化比较能力(Comparisons)"和"在多元文化社区中学以致用的能力(Communities)"。

　　《成长》分三级。每级有十个单元，可以在一个学年内完成。教材所应用的教学方法是循序渐进的，能帮助学生从最基本、简单的表达，慢慢提升到更长、更复杂的表达。和传统教材以"生词－课文－语法"为中心的教学方法不同，《成长》每一个单元的内容根据交际目标分解成几个大步骤，每个大步骤下面又有几个小步骤，这样既能降低初学者的学习难度，又能让学生打好基础、不断巩固所学。每一单元都经过了精心设计，同时融合了人际交往的三种模式(语言沟通、理解诠释、表达演示)。

　　教材还在课文和活动中融入了许多中国传统与现代的文化内容，让学生可以更深入地了解中国、中国人、中国文化和中国习俗。课本里也安排了许多美国人熟悉的人物和场景，能够激发学生对用中文解释自己的本土文化产生兴趣。为了强化语言学习的效果，编者还在语言教学和其他学科之间设置了许多有意义的联系。

　　《成长》每一级教材都有课本和练习册。课本每单元开篇清楚列明学习目标，并通过热身活动导入正题。每个单元有三至四个主要教学步骤和交际目标。每个步骤都有一个生词表、语法解释、相关文化知识和练习。在主要步骤之后，设有阅读篇章、对话、综合练习、趣味活动，让学生能够延伸学习。单元末还列出该单元所介绍的所有生词和句型，以及一个自我评估表。课本附录则包括中英生词索引、主要句型表和中国地图。

　　练习册包括形式多样的练习题，有助于培养学生听、说、读、写等各方面的能力。听力练习通过录音片段训练学生的听力理解能力。情景活动培养学生在沟通交际和演示交际方面的口语表达能力。多样化的阅读篇章(对话、短文、书信、告示、电邮等)有助于培养学生的阅读理解能力。除此之外，在书写能力方面，学生会练习以正确的笔顺书写生字词，并用中文回答各种形式的问题，例如简单的填充题以及更具挑战性的自由题。

　　教材还配有专门的学习网站(http://stepup.cengageasia.com)，提供汉语拼音总表、互动式词卡、课本和练习册录音(mp3)、额外的网上练习以及教师辅助资源(包括教师手册、课本和练习册录音稿和参考答案等等)。

　　《成长》可让学生积极、有效地学习中文，掌握应用中文的技能，并培养他们终身学习中文的兴趣。

Acknowledgements

We would like to thank the following people for their valuable comments and suggestions during the product development stage of *Step Up with Chinese*.

- **JIANHUA BAI**
  Professor of Chinese
  Kenyon College, Ohio

- **NING CHEN**
  Laurel School, Ohio

- **XING KING**
  The Bishop's School, California

- **JIE LEI**
  George C. Marshall High School,
  Fairfax County Public Schools, Virginia

- **LI LI**
  Potomac Elementary School, Maryland

- **LIHUA LI**
  Berkeley Preparatory School, Florida

- **FEI REED**
  Sidwell Friends Middle School,
  Washington, D.C.

- **ADAM ROSS**
  Lakeside School, Washington

- **PHYLLIS ZHANG**
  George Washington University, Washington D.C.

- **LESLIE O. ZIMRING**
  Supervisor, World Languages & Bilingual Education
  Summit School District, New Jersey

CONTENTS

成长 - STEP UP WITH CHINESE

Introduction 1	Pinyin	拼音
Introduction 2	Chinese Characters	汉字

交际目标 Communicative Goals	主要步骤 Main Steps	核心词汇 Core Vocabulary	语言点 Language Focus
1 ◈ **Nice to meet you!**		**你好！**	
◆ 打招呼 Greeting People	**Step 1** 打招呼 Greeting People	1. 人称代词 Proper nouns	1. 你好！/ 你们好！
◆ 介绍自己和他人 Introducing yourself and others	**Step 2** 介绍自己和他人 Making Introductions	2. 问候语 Greetings	2. 我是小伟。 他是马丁。
◆ 问候他人 Asking how people are	**Step 3** 问候他人 Asking How People Are	3. 主要姓氏 Chinese surnames	3. 你/他是谁？ 我/他是王小伟。
◆ 询问姓名 Asking for someone's name and surname	**Step 4** 询问姓名 Asking Someone's Name		4. 你好吗？ 我很好。/ 还可以。
			5. 你忙吗？ 我很忙/ 不忙。
			6. 你叫什么(名字)？ 我叫罗伯特。
			7. 你/您姓什么？ 我姓李。
2 ◈ **Getting to know you**		**你是哪国人？**	
◆ 问国籍 Asking and telling one's nationality	**Step 1** 国籍 About One's Nationality	1. 国籍 Nationalities	1. 你是哪国人？ 我是美国人。
◆ 问家乡 Discussing one's hometown	**Step 2** 家乡 About One's Hometown	2. 国家与城市 Countries and cities	2. 你是中国人吗？ 对，我是中国人。/ 不是，我是英国人。
◆ 问家在哪儿 Asking and telling where one lives	**Step 3** 住址 About Where One Lives	3. 方位 Directions	3. 她也是美国人吗？ 对，我们都是美国人。
			4. 你是哪里人？ 我是上海人。
			5. 你家在哪儿？ 我家在北京。
			6. 你住哪儿？ 我住南边。

SCOPE & SEQUENCE

文化知识 Cultural Knowledge	贯连和比较 Connections and Comparisons	任务和实践 Tasks and Community Applications
		20
1. 不同文化中的问候方式 Greetings around the world 2. 英文中的中文词语 Chinese words used in English 3. 对不同人的问候方式 The proper ways to greet different people 4. 称呼中国人 Addressing a Chinese person 5. 中国人的姓和名 Chinese names	社会学 Social Studies: • 世界不同文化中的问候 Greetings in different cultures • 人类各语言中称呼爸爸妈妈的相似性 Similar pronunciation for Papa and Mama in different cultures 比较 Comparison: • 中文和英文中疑问词的不同位置 The placement of question words in Chinese and English • 中英姓名的不同 Differences between Chinese and English names	1. 小组活动：打招呼并自我介绍，然后问同学的名字 Group Work: Greet classmates and introduce your name, then ask the names of your classmates. 2. 为自己和家人取中文名字 Give yourself and your family members Chinese names. 3. 在网页上放照片并自我介绍 Make a home page with a picture of yourself. Write a caption to greet viewers and introduce yourself to them.
		48
1. 家和家乡 The Chinese concept of hometown 2. 北京和上海 Beijing and Shanghai 3. 中国和其他国家的名人 Celebrities from China and other countries 4. 中国身份证特点 Features of a Chinese ID card	地理 Geography: • 各国国旗 National flags of different countries • 中国名城 Major cities of China • 世界名城 Famous cities around the world	1. 写下十位名人的名字、性别、国籍 Write down the names, gender and nationalities of ten celebrities. 2. 访问：向同学问询名字、国籍、家乡和住址，写一篇简单介绍，然后和全班分享 Interview: Ask your classmate his/her name, nationality, hometown and place of residence. Write a short introduction and present to the class. 3. 情景演练：打招呼，问名字、国籍、家乡和住址，然后道别 Skit: Greet your classmate and ask his/her name, nationality, hometown and where he/she lives and studies, and then say good-bye.

IX

交际目标 Communicative Goals	主要步骤 Main Steps	核心词汇 Core Vocabulary	语言点 Language Focus

3 ❖ What time is it?   现在几点？

交际目标	主要步骤	核心词汇	语言点
◆ 数字的表达 Counting and saying numbers ◆ 小数的表达 Reading numbers with decimals ◆ 序数的表达 Stating ordinal numbers ◆ 一天中不同时段的表达 Talking about different segments of a day ◆ 询问时间 Asking and telling time	Step 1 个、十、百、千、万位数 Counting and Saying Numbers Step 2 小数、序数 Different Types of Numbers Step 3 一天的不同时段 Different Segments of a Day Step 4 询问时间 Asking and Telling Time	1. 个、十、百、千、万位数 One to five-digit numbers 2. 小数、序数 Decimals and ordinal numbers 3. 时段 Different segments of a day 4. 时间 Time (hour, minutes, seconds)	1. 整数、小数、序数的表达 2. 不同时段的表达 3. 现在几点？ 现在三点。 4. 现在三点十分。 5. 现在三点零五(分)。 6. 现在两点一刻。 7. 现在三点半。 8. 现在差一刻四点。

4 ❖ What's today's date?   今天几号？

交际目标	主要步骤	核心词汇	语言点
◆ 表达年、月、星期、日 Talking about the year, month, week and day ◆ 时间段的表达 Stating a specific period of time ◆ 问年龄与生日 Asking someone's age and birthday ◆ 使用疑问句"你呢?" Using tag questions ◆ 表达祝福 Expressing well wishes	Step 1 年、月、星期、日 Year, Month, Week and Day Step 2 年、月、星期、日的时间段 Counting Years, Months, Weeks and Days Step 3 年龄与生日 Age and Birthday	1. 年、月、日、星期 Year, months, days and weeks 2. 年龄、生日 Age and birthday	1. 今年是2011年。 2. 一月、二月、三月…… 3. 今天几号? 今天二月五号。 4. 今天星期几? 今天星期五。 5. 上个月; 下个星期…… 6. 三年; 七天…… 7. 两个月; 四个星期 8. 你多大? / 你几岁? 9. 我的生日是一月三号。 你呢? 10. 祝你生日快乐!

文化知识 Cultural Knowledge	贯连和比较 Connections and Comparisons	任务和实践 Tasks and Community Applications

70

1. 中国的吉利数字 Lucky numbers in Chinese culture 2. 算盘 The Chinese abacus 3. 九九乘法表 The Chinese multiplication table 4. 中文里表达时间的顺序 Sequence of telling time in Chinese 5. 中国数字手语 Chinese hand gestures for numbers	数学 Mathematics: • 整数、小数 Integers and decimals • 看钟表说时间 Telling time • 圆周率 The value of Pi • 乘法表 The multiplication table 旅游 Travel: • 中国紧急号码 Emergency numbers in China 地理 Geography: • 中国的时区 Time zone in China 比较 Comparison: • 中英表达时间顺序的不同 Sequence of telling time in Chinese and English	1. 读电话号码、邮编、车牌号 Read aloud telephone numbers, postal codes and car license numbers in Chinese. 2. 用中文说价格 State prices in Chinese. 3. 制作每日作息表，用中文写时间 Work out your daily schedule in Chinese.

98

1. 中国农历 The Chinese lunar calendar 2. 象形文字月和日 The evolution of pictographic characters 月 and 日 3. 向中国人问询年龄 The proper way to ask a Chinese person's age 4. 常用中文祝语 Common Chinese expressions of good wishes 5. 中国节日的日期 Dates of major Chinese festivals 6. 二十四节气 The 24 solar terms	天文与地理 Astronomy and Geography: • 二十四节气 The 24 solar terms 比较 Comparison: • 阳历与阴历 The Gregorian calendar and the Chinese lunar calendar • 年月日在中英文中的表达 Telling dates in Chinese and English • 中西文化中对问询年龄的差异 Difference between Chinese and Western cultures: when asking someone's age.	1. 看中国火车票说日期 Telling time, dates and other departure and arrival information from a Chinese train ticket. 2. 搜寻中国重要节日的相关内容 Research and discover important facts of some Chinese festivals. 3. 制作生日年历，写上全班同学的生日 Mark the birthdays of all your classmates on your birthday calendar. 4. 制作生日卡，写上中英文祝语，送给社区老人院 Make birthday cards with Chinese and English well wishes for the elderly.

交际目标 Communicative Goals	主要步骤 Main Steps	核心词汇 Core Vocabulary	语言点 Language Focus

5 ◈ My family　　　我们一家人

◆ 介绍家庭成员 Talking about one's family	**Step 1** **家庭成员** About One's Family	1. 家庭成员 Family members	1. 这是谁? 这是我爸爸。
◆ 谈家庭人口 Stating the size of a family	**Step 2** **家庭人口** Number of Members in a Family	2. 身体部位 Parts of the body	2. 这是你爸爸吗? 对 / 不是。
◆ 介绍兄弟姐妹 Talking about one's siblings	**Step 3** **介绍兄弟姐妹** Introducing One's Siblings		3. 你家有几口人? 我家有三口人。
◆ 形容人物 Describing people	**Step 4** **形容人物** Describing People		4. 爸爸、妈妈和我。
			5. 你有哥哥吗? 有。我有一个哥哥。
			6. 你有没有姐姐? 我没有姐姐。
			7. 我的头发。 我的耳朵。
			8. 我爸爸很高。

6 ◈ My family pet　　　我家的宠物

◆ 介绍动物名称 Identifying animals in Chinese	**Step 1** **各种动物** Types of Animals and Pets	1. 动物名 Names ot animals	1. 这是什么动物? 这是牛。
◆ 表达对动物的喜恶 Expressing likes and dislikes for animals	**Step 2** **表达对动物的喜恶** Expressing Likes and Dislikes	2. 量词 (动物) Measure words for animals	2. 动物园有什么动物? 动物园有熊猫, 还有狮子。
◆ 谈动物和宠物 Talking about animals and pets	**Step 3** **表达动物的数量** Counting Animals	3. 动物动作 Terms describing how animals move	3. 我喜欢狗, 也喜欢猫, 不喜欢蛇。
◆ 描述动物的动作 Describing how animals move	**Step 4** **动物的动作** How Animals Move		4. 你喜欢不喜欢猫? 我喜欢猫。
			5. 我最喜欢狗, 最不喜欢猫。
			6. 一只狗, 两条蛇, 六头牛, 八匹马
			7. 你家有没有小狗? 有, 我家有一只小狗。
			8. 乌龟爬, 兔子跳, 鸟儿飞。

文化知识 Cultural Knowledge	贯连和比较 Connections and Comparisons	任务和实践 Tasks and Community Applications

126

1. 中国人的家庭观念 Kinship in Chinese culture 2. 中国家庭里的亲属称谓 Terms of address in the Chinese family 3. "口"与"人口" 口 - a reference to population 4. 中国家谱 Chinese genealogy	科学 Science: • 人体部位 Parts of the body 社会学 Sociology: • 家谱 Chinese genealogy 文学 Literature: • 《红楼梦》 Dream of the Red Chamber 比较 Comparison: • 中国家庭和西方家庭结构 Chinese and Western family structure	1. 绘制家庭树，并注上称呼、姓名、年龄、生日 Create a family tree and label each member with the name, age and birthday. 2. 看同学全家福，逐个询问其家人 Look at a family photo of your classmate and ask questions about his/her family members. 3. 小组活动：扮演不同"家庭"角色，介绍并形容自己 Group Work: Play the role of a "family member." Introduce and describe this member (age, height and general appearance) to the class in Chinese.

148

1. 中国和其他国家常见的宠物 Pets in China and other countries 2. 大熊猫 The giant panda 3. 中国的龙和凤 The Chinese dragon and phoenix 4. 北京动物园和美国国家动物园 Beijing Zoo and the National Zoo of U.S.A 5. 十二生肖 The twelve zodiac animals	生物 Biology: • 濒危动物——大熊猫 Endangered animal: The giant panda 数学 Mathematics: • 各国宠物的数据 Statistics of the number of pets in different countries	1. 调查：同学有没有宠物，是什么宠物，叫什么名字 Survey: Find out if your classmates have any pets, and the names of their pets. 2. 做宠物图书，介绍宠物来自哪里，叫什么名字，并形容它 Create a four-page scrapbook to introduce your pet with pictures and captions. 3. 小组活动：看动物园导游图，计划园内行程 Group Work: Study the map of a zoo and plan a walk-about route for a tour.

交际目标 Communicative Goals	主要步骤 Main Steps	核心词汇 Core Vocabulary	语言点 Language Focus

7 My school 我的学校

Communicative Goals	Main Steps	Core Vocabulary	Language Focus
◆ 介绍学校设施 Introducing school facilities ◆ 形容位置 Describing locations ◆ 介绍教室里的东西及 其颜色 Describing classroom items and their colors ◆ 谈论课程 Talking about school courses	Step 1 介绍学校 Describing One's School Step 2 介绍教室 Describing One's Classroom Step 3 谈课程 Talking About Courses and Classes	1. 学校设施 School facilities 2. 方位词 Location words 3. 教室布置 Classroom items 4. 文具 School supplies 5. 量词 (文具) Measure words for stationery 6. 颜色 Colors 7. 学科名 Names of courses	1. 学校里有什么? 学校里有一个图书馆。 2. 图书馆在哪儿? 图书馆在教学楼(的)后边。 3. 你家离学校远不远? 我家离学校很远。 4. 墙上有什么? 墙上有(一张)地图。 5. 量词：个，支，块，把， 张、瓶 6. 我有一个红色的书包。 7. 借我一支笔，行吗? 行，给你。 8. 你有什么课? 我有中文课。 9. 你有几门课? 我有八门课。 10. 你学过法语吗? 我学过法语。

8 My busy schedule 天天都很忙

Communicative Goals	Main Steps	Core Vocabulary	Language Focus
◆ 谈课表 Talking about one's class schedule ◆ 介绍一天中的活动 Describing one's daily routine ◆ 谈课外活动 Talking about after-school activities ◆ 谈论活动时间与地点 Expressing where and when one does an activity	Step 1 课程表 About One's Class Schedule Step 2 课程的不同时段与顺序 More About One's Class Schedule Step 3 每日活动 About One's Daily Schedule	1. 日常生活 Daily routine 2. 休闲活动 Leisure activities	1. 你今天有什么课? 我今天有中文课。 2. 你今天有几节课? 我今天有六节课。 3. 今天几点上课? 今天早上八点上课。 4. 九点以前是什么课? 三点以后有什么课? 5. 从早上八点到九点我有 历史课。 6. 你几点起床? 我早上七点半起床。 7. 你在哪儿上课? 我在教室上课。 8. 昨天晚上你做什么了? 我上网了。

文化知识 Cultural Knowledge	贯连和比较 Connections and Comparisons	任务和实践 Tasks and Community Applications

168

1. 中美教育制度
Educational systems in China and the United States

2. 中国的班级制
Classroom system in China

3. 高考
China's National College Entrance Examination

数学 Mathematics:
- 各学科人数统计表
Statistics of the number of students taking different subjects

看地图 Map Reading:
- 表达方位
Specifying relative locations

比较 Comparison:
- 中美教育制度
Educational systems in China and the United States

1. 在校园简图上为各种设施标上名字，回答问题
Label each building on a school map and answer the questions.

2. 写校园简介，包括校园设施、师生人数、班级数量
Write a short introduction about your school describing its facilities, enrollment and the types of courses offered.

3. 统计每个科目的学生人数，制成图表
Work out a graph to show the class sizes for each subject.

192

1. 中国中学生的课程表
Class schedule of a typical Chinese middle school

2. 中国英语热
English language learning in China

3. 中国学校的课外活动
Extracurricular activities in schools in China

4. 课间操和眼保健操
Daily morning and eye exercises practiced in schools in China

健康 Health Education:
- 课间操和眼保健操
Morning exercises and ocular exercises in schools in China

比较 Comparison:
- 中美中学生的课程表
Class schedules of Chinese and American middle school students
- 中美中学生的课外活动
Extracurricular activities in schools in China and the U.S.

1. 制作一周课程表，列出时间和科目
Work out a class schedule and list the time and subjects.

2. 制作一张符合高考要求的课程表，然后用十句话加以描述
Make a schedule that meets the requirement of China's National College Entrance Exam and then describe it with at least five sentences.

3. 写一则网志描述你在学校里的一天
Write a blog entry describing a day in your school.

4. 访问同学并记录他们的一天，然后在班上总结汇报
Interview your classmates about their daily routines. Report your findings to the class.

XV

SCOPE AND SEQUENCE

交际目标 Communicative Goals	主要步骤 Main Steps	核心词汇 Core Vocabulary	语言点 Language Focus

9 ◇ My interests, my dreams 　　我的爱好

◆ 谈爱好 Talking about one's interests and hobbies	Step 1 爱好 About One's Interests and Hobbies	1. 爱好 Hobbies	1. 你有什么爱好? 我喜欢游泳。
◆ 能力的表达 Talking about one's abilities and skills	Step 2 能力 About One's Abilities and Skills	2. 体育运动 Sports	2. 你的爱好是什么? 我的爱好是唱歌。
◆ 谈梦想 Stating one's dream job	Step 3 梦想 About One's Dreams and Aspirations		3. 你会打网球吗? 会。/ 不会。
◆ 描述花在爱好上的时间 Exchanging information about time spent on hobbies			4. 他打乒乓球打得很好。
			5. 我想当运动员。
			6. 我天天跑步。

10 ◇ It tastes so good! 　　好吃!

◆ 谈食物与饮料 Talking about foods and beverages	Step 1 谈食物及其味道 Talking About Foods and How They Taste	1. 水果 Fruits	1. 你吃什么? 我吃饺子。
◆ 形容食物的味道 Describing the taste of various foods	Step 2 表达对食物的喜好 Expressing Food Preferences	2. 蔬菜 Vegetables	2. 你喝什么? 我喝中国茶。
◆ 表达对食物的喜恶与选择 Expressing food preferences	Step 3 点菜 Ordering Food	3. 海鲜 Seafood	3. 汉堡好吃吗? 汉堡很好吃。
◆ 选择疑问句 Asking choice-type questions		4. 肉类 Meats	4. 可乐好喝吗? 可乐很好喝。
◆ 点菜 Ordering food		5. 饮料 Beverages	5. 西瓜很甜。 咖啡很苦。
		6. 中式菜单 Chinese menu	6. 我喜欢吃饺子,也喜欢吃热狗。
		7. 西式菜单 Western menu	7. 你要吃什么? 我要吃炒饭。
		8. 味道 Tastes	8. 你要吃饺子还是油条?
		9. 量词 (食品和饮料) Measure words for common dishes and beverages	9. 你要点什么菜? 来一碗面,再来一杯水。

文化知识 Cultural Knowledge	贯连和比较 Connections and Comparisons	任务和实践 Tasks and Community Applications

1. 中国 "国球" 乒乓球 Ping pong diplomacy 2. 文人四艺 The four arts of a Chinese scholar 3. 太极拳 The origin and key characteristics of *Taiji*	**历史 History:** • 乒乓外交 China-U.S. ping pong diplomacy **体育 Physical Education:** • 奥运会体育项目 Different sports and games played during the most recent Olympics Games **比较 Comparison:** • 在中国和美国受欢迎的体育项目 Popular sports in China and the U.S.	1. 根据各自的爱好进行才艺表演，并制作全班才艺表 Act out your hobbies in class and record the hobbies of classmates. 2. 搜索一个和你有共同爱好的名人的资料，然后和全班分享 Research a famous person who shares the same interest or hobby with you. Present what you have found to the class. 3. 搜索关于两个奥运会金牌得主的资料，然后在班上汇报 Research two gold medalists at the Olympic Games and present your findings to the class. 4. 访问至少五位同学，看他们花在爱好方面的时间有多少 Find out from at least five classmates how often and how much time they spend on their hobbies.

1. 中国水果 Fruits grown in China 2. 常见中国菜与饮料 Popular Chinese dishes and beverages 3. 洋快餐在中国 Fast-food in China 4. 筷子的历史 History of chopsticks 5. 食物在中国文化中的象征意义 Food symbolism in Chinese culture 6. 中餐里上菜的顺序 Order of courses in a Chinese meal	**健康 Health Education:** • 食物金字塔 The food pyramid **比较 Comparison:** • 中国和美国特有的蔬菜和水果 Fruits and vegetables native to China and the US • 水果在不同文化中的象征意义 The symbolic meaning of fruits in different cultures • 中西餐里上菜的顺序 Order of courses in Chinese and Western cuisines	1. 调查食堂里的食物与饮料是否合学生口味 Do a survey to find out whether the foods and drinks served in the school cafeteria suit students' tastes. 2. 调查并记录全班同学最喜欢的食物和饮料 Interview your classmates and record their favorite foods and beverages. 3. 为家人准备晚餐，拟出三道菜以及所需要的食材 Plan a simple dinner for your family. Write down three dishes you would like to prepare and the ingredients needed. 4. 情景演练：看菜单并向餐馆侍者点菜 Skit: Reading a menu and ordering food in a restaurant from a waiter.

拼音
Pinyin

hànzì
Xiànzài jǐ diǎn
Nǐ shì nǎguórén
Wǒ jiā de chǒngwù   Wǒ de xuéxiào
Jīntiān jǐ hào   Wǒmen yì jiā rén
Nǐ hǎo

What is *Pinyin*?

Chinese is not a phonetic language. The pronunciation is not related to the writing of Chinese words (characters). *Pinyin* (that helps in pronouncing the sounds) is a way to transcribe Chinese characters so people can pronounce it. The writing of *pinyin* is sometimes similar to the English alphabet.

Pinyin is a romanized system for pronouncing Chinese characters. In Chinese, each character represents a syllable, which can be spelled and pronounced using the *pinyin* system.

There are three basic elements in *pinyin*: **Initials**, **Finals**, and **Tones**. Most Chinese syllables can be spelled with one initial followed by one final, with a tone mark to indicate the tone.

Example:

人	Initial	Final	Tone	*Pinyin*
	r	en	/	rén

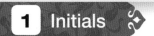

1 Initials

Audio Most Chinese syllables begin with an initial. There are 21 initials in *pinyin*:

b	p	m	f	d	t	n	l	g	k
BAL	PORE	MORE	FOR	DIRTY	TERMINATE	NURSE	LEARN	YOGURT	CURT

sound like . . . ⟶

(For reference only. Refer to audio recording for standard pronunciation.)

h	j	q	x	z*	c*	s*	zh*	ch*	sh*	r*
HER	JEEP	CHEESE	SHEEP	ADDS	ITS	SAY	KNOWLEDGE	CHILLY	SHY	RAZOR

sound like . . . ⟶

* "z," "c," "s," "zh," "ch," "sh" and "r" can form syllables on their own without any finals, and are written as "zi," "ci," "si," "zhi," "chi" and "ri" respectively. Though their written forms contain an "i," the "i" sound is not pronounced.

2 Finals

Audio There are 36 finals, which can be divided into two types:

A. Simple finals

A simple final contains only one vowel. There are 6 of them:

a	o	e	i*	u*	ü*
FATHER	MORE	FUR	TEA	MOOD	PNEUMONIA

sound like . . . ⟶

* When no initials are present, "i," "u" and "ü" are spelled "yi," "wu" and "yu" respectively, and "ü" is written as "u" after j, q or x.

B. Compound finals

These are finals with two or more vowels or consonants. They can be further divided into four categories.

1. Finals beginning with "a," "o" or "e"

ai	ei	ao	ou	er	an	en	ang	eng	ong
AISLE	PLAY	COW	GO	GIRL	MAN	OPEN	HUNG	FERN	JOHN

sound like . . . ⟶

2. Finals beginning with "i"

ia	ie	iao	iou	in	ian	ing	iang	iong
"YA"	YES	YOWL	YO-YO	BIN	YEN	FINGER	YOUNG	JUNG

sound like . . . ⟶

When "in" and "ing" form syllables on their own, "y" must be added in front of these finals:

in ⟶ yin   ing ⟶ ying

When "ia," "ie," "iao," "iou," "ian," "iang" and "iong" form syllables on their own, the vowel "i" must be written as "y":

ia ⟶ ya   ie ⟶ ye   iao ⟶ yao   iou ⟶ you

ian ⟶ yan   iang ⟶ yang   iong ⟶ yong

3. Finals beginning with "u"

ua	uo	uai	uei	uan	uen	uang	ueng
GUAVA	WAR	SWIPE	WEIGH	SWAN	TRUANT	WANGLE	WENDY

sound like . . . ⟶

When these finals form syllables on their own, the vowel "u" must be written as "w":

ua ⟶ wa   uo ⟶ wo   uai ⟶ wai   uei ⟶ wei

uan ⟶ wan   uen ⟶ wen   uang ⟶ wang   ueng ⟶ weng

4. Finals beginning with "ü"

üe	üan	ün
YURT	YUAN	WIN

sound like . . . ⟶

When these finals form syllables on their own, "y" must be added in front of them, and the two dots above "u" must be removed:

üe ⟶ yue   üan ⟶ yuan   ün ⟶ yun

In some cases, the syllable only contains a final:

an　en　ou
安　恩　欧

The next 2 pages show a *pinyin* table listing all the possible combinations of initials and finals. Try pronouncing them with your teacher.

PINYIN TABLE
Combination of initials and finals
汉语拼音声母韵母拼合总表

Finals	1	2	3	4	5	6	7	8	9	10	11	12	13	14	15	16	17	18
	a	o	e	ai	ei	ao	ou	er	an	en	ang	eng	ong	i	ia	iao	ie	iou*
Initials														yi	ya	yao	ye	you
1 b	ba	bo		bai	bei	bao			ban	ben	bang	beng		bi		biao	bie	
2 p	pa	po		pai	pei	pao	pou		pan	pen	pang	peng		pi		piao	pie	
3 m	ma	mo	me	mai	mei	mao	mou		man	men	mang	meng		mi		miao	mie	miu
4 f	fa	fo			fei		fou		fan	fen	fang	feng						
5 d	da		de	dai	dei	dao	dou		dan		dang	deng	dong	di		diao	die	diu
6 t	ta		te	tai		tao	tou		tan		tang	teng	tong	ti		tiao	tie	
7 n	na		ne	nai	nei	nao	nou		nan	nen	nang	neng	nong	ni		niao	nie	niu
8 l	la		le	lai	lei	lao	lou		lan		lang	leng	long	li	lia	liao	lie	liu
9 g	ga		ge	gai	gei	gao	gou		gan	gen	gang	geng	gong					
10 k	ka		ke	kai	kei	kao	kou		kan	ken	kang	keng	kong					
11 h	ha		he	hai	hei	hao	hou		han	hen	hang	heng	hong					
12 j														ji	jia	jiao	jie	jiu
13 q														qi	qia	qiao	qie	qiu
14 x														xi	xia	xiao	xie	xiu
15 zh	zha		zhe	zhai	zhei	zhao	zhou		zhan	zhen	zhang	zheng	zhong	zhi				
16 ch	cha		che	chai		chao	chou		chan	chen	chang	cheng	chong	chi				
17 sh	sha		she	shai	shei	shao	shou		shan	shen	shang	sheng		shi				
18 r			re			rao	rou		ran	ren	rang	reng	rong	ri				
19 z	za		ze	zai		zao	zou		zan	zen	zang	zeng	zong	zi				
20 c	ca		ce	cai		cao	cou		can	cen	cang	ceng	cong	ci				
21 s	sa		se	sai		sao	sou		san	sen	sang	seng	song	si				

19	20	21	22	23	24	25	26	27	28	29	30	31	32	33	34	35	36
ian	in	iang	ing	iong	u	ua	uo*	uai	uei*	uan	uen*	uang	ueng	ü	üe	üan	ün
yan	yin	yang	ying	yong	wu	wa	wo	wai	wei	wan	wen	wang	weng	yu	yue	yuan	yun
bian	bin		bing		bu												
pian	pin		ping		pu												
mian	min		ming		mu												
					fu												
dian			ding		du		duo		dui	duan	dun						
tian			ting		tu		tuo		tui	tuan	tun						
nian	nin	niang	ning		nu		nuo			nuan				nü	nüe		
lian	lin	liang	ling		lu		luo			luan	lun			lü	lüe		
					gu	gua	guo	guai	gui	guan	gun	guang					
					ku	kua	kuo	kuai	kui	kuan	kun	kuang					
					hu	hua	huo	huai	hui	huan	hun	huang					
jian	jin	jiang	jing	jiong										ju	jue	juan	jun
qian	qin	qiang	qing	qiong										qu	que	quan	qun
xian	xin	xiang	xing	xiong										xu	xue	xuan	xun
					zhu	zhua	zhuo	zhuai	zhui	zhuan	zhun	zhuang					
					chu	chua	chuo	chuai	chui	chuan	chun	chuang					
					shu	shua	shuo	shuai	shui	shuan	shun	shuang					
					ru	rua	ruo		rui	ruan	run						
					zu		zuo		zui	zuan	zun						
					cu		cuo		cui	cuan	cun						
					su		suo		sui	suan	sun						

3 Tones

A. The four tones

The third element in *pinyin* is tone. There are four tones in *pinyin*, all written above one of the vowels in a final:

The first tone is a flat or high level tone that is represented by ▬

The second tone is a rising tone represented by ⟋

The third tone is a falling-rising tone represented by ⌄

The fourth tone is a high-falling tone represented by ⟍

On the right is a *pinyin* tone chart that shows the relative changes in pitch for the four tones:

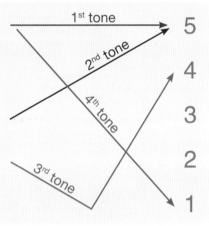

B. Placement of tone marks

The tone mark is placed on the vowel in the final. Here is an example of how the four tones are marked:

bā	bá	bǎ	bà
1st tone	2nd tone	3rd tone	4th tone

When the tone mark is placed on the vowel "i," remove the dot above.

For example: jī, jí, jǐ, jì.

When there are two or more vowels in the final, the tone mark is placed on the main vowel, i.e., the vowel that requires the mouth to be open the widest when pronouncing.

For example: nǎi, gǒu, yuè, liù, shuǐ.

Here are some useful guidelines for the placement of tone marks.

1. If there is an "a," mark on it.

   Example: māo, máo, mǎo, mào

2. If there is no "a," but "o" or "e" is present, mark on either of these two letters. "o" and "e" will not appear at the same time.

   Examples: lōu, lóu, lǒu, lòu
   xiē, xié, xiě, xiè

3. If there is no "o" or "e," mark on "i," "u" or "ü." If "i" and "u" appear at the same time, the tone mark goes on the second vowel.

   Examples: niū, niú, niǔ, niù
   suī, suí, suǐ, suì

C. The neutral tone

In addition to the above four tones, there is a neutral tone, which is read quickly and lightly. It has no tone mark.

Examples:

bàba	māma	gēge	jiějie
爸爸	妈妈	哥哥	姐姐
father	mother	elder brother	elder sister

Tones in *pinyin* help to differentiate words with different meanings. The same combination of finals and initials can represent different meanings when they have different tones. Consider the syllable "ba":

bā	bá	bǎ	bà
八	拔	靶	爸
eight	pull out	target	father

D. Tone changes

In Chinese, the tone of a word sometimes changes, depending on the tone of the word that precedes or follows it. There are three main circumstances that require tone changes.

1. If a third tone precedes a third tone, the first third tone becomes a second tone.

    Example: 你好 (níhǎo, hello)

    When pronounced together, 你 takes the second tone and 好 remains in the third tone.

    If the third tone is followed by any tone other than the third tone, it changes to a half third tone, which falls and does not rise in pitch.

    Examples: 老师 (lǎoshī, teacher)
    以前 (yǐqián, before)
    美丽 (měilì, beautiful)

2. The word 不 takes the fourth tone, but when it is followed by another fourth tone, it becomes second tone.

    Examples: 不是 (búshì, not)
    不要 (búyào, don't want)

3. The word 一 is first tone when it refers to the number "one." If it precedes first, second, or third tones, it takes the fourth tone.

    Examples: 一天 (yìtiān, one day)
    一年 (yìnián, one year)
    一口 (yìkǒu, one mouthful)

    If it precedes a fourth tone, it takes the second tone.

    Examples: 一半 (yíbàn, half)
    一路 (yílù, the whole journey)

E. The suffix 儿

Very often in Chinese, especially in the Beijing dialect, some words are pronounced with the suffix 儿 (er). The suffix does not change the meaning of the word it attaches to. In written form, the suffix is spelled r, placed after the word is attached to.

Examples:

zhèr	nàr	huàr	dāor
这儿	那儿	画儿	刀儿
here	there	drawing	knife

1. Practice pronouncing the following initials and finals with your teacher:

   ❶ Initials: b, p, m, f

   ❷ Finals: a, o, e, i, u, ü

2. Read aloud the following syllables in four tones with your teacher.

   ❶ ā á ǎ à   ❹ yī yí yǐ yì

   ❷ ō ó ǒ ò   ❺ wū wú wǔ wù

   ❸ ē é ě è   ❻ yū yú yǔ yù

3. Below are some combinations of finals and initials with the four tones. Practice pronouncing them in the four tones with your teacher.

   bā bá bǎ bà   bō bó bǒ bò

   pā pá pǎ pà   pō pó pǒ pò

   mā má mǎ mà   mō mó mǒ mò

   fā fá fǎ fà   fū fú fǔ fù

4. Read aloud the following words with neutral tones.

   ❶ wǒmen   我们 (we)   ❹ běnzi   本子 (notebook)

   ❷ dìdi   弟弟 (younger brother) ❺ mèimei   妹妹 (younger sister)

   ❸ péngyou   朋友 (friend)   ❻ yuèliang   月亮 (moon)

5. Practice pronouncing the syllables below, paying attention to changes in the third tone.

   hěnlěng   shuǐguǒ   shǒubiǎo   zuǒshǒu   xǐzǎo

6. Practice pronouncing the syllables below, paying attention to the pronunciation of the suffix "r."

   ❶ niǎor   ❹ xiǎogǒur   ❼ bīnggùnr

   ❷ huār   ❺ miàntiáor   ❽ xiǎoháir

   ❸ huàr   ❻ xiǎomāor   ❾ yǎnjìngr

汉字
Chinese Characters

现在几点

我们一家人　我家的宠物　我的学校

你好　我的爱好

好吃!

Chinese characters represent the oldest continuously used system of writing in the world. For thousands of years, they have made remarkable contributions to the Chinese language and culture. They have also significantly influenced other East Asian languages such as Japanese, Korean and Vietnamese.

The number of Chinese characters was about 47,035 during the 18th and 19th centuries, but less than a quarter of these characters are now in common use. Studies have shown that full literacy in the Chinese language requires a knowledge of only three to four thousand characters.

1 The evolution of Chinese characters

Chinese characters originated at the end of the Shang Dynasty (c. 1600 B.C. – 1046 B.C.), and were initially derived from oracle bone inscriptions.

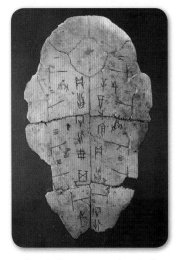
Inscription on a tortoise shell

Inscription on an ox bone

Later they were carved on bronze objects (c. 1400 B.C. – 221 B.C.), standardized as seal scripts (c. 221 B.C. – 25 A.D.), and became regular scripts (25 A.D. – present). Below are two characters 水 (water) and 火 (fire) that illustrate the evolution of the Chinese characters.

| shuǐ 水 water | oracle bone script → inscription on bronze objects → seal script → regular script 水 |
| huǒ 火 fire | oracle bone script → inscription on bronze objects → seal script → regular script 火 |

2 Formation of characters

Chinese characters can be divided into six categories, each representing a method of formation. Among them, pictograms, ideogrammic compounds and phono-semantic compounds are the three common categories that most characters fall into.

A. Pictograms (象形字, xiàngxíngzì)

About 4% of Chinese characters are derived directly from individual pictograms. They depict the shapes of objects perceived in nature and in daily life.

Over the years, these characters have been standardized, simplified and stylized to make writing easier, and their derivation is therefore not always obvious. Compare the following pictograms with today's forms to see the link.

B. Ideogrammic Compounds (会意字, huìyìzì)

About 13% of characters fall into this category. These characters symbolically combine pictograms or ideograms to create a new character that represents the meaning of its components. For instance, doubling the pictogram 木 (mù, tree) produces 林 (lín, grove), while tripling it produces 森 (sēn, forest).

木　　林　　森

Similarly, 明 (míng, bright) is formed by combining 日 (rì, sun) and 月 (yuè, moon), the two natural sources of light:

Other common examples include the characters 休 (xiū, rest), composed of the pictograms 人 (rén, person) and 木 (mù, tree), and also 好 (hǎo, good), composed of the pictograms 女 (nǚ), daughter) and 子(zǐ, son).

C. Phono-semantic Compounds (形声字, xíngshēngzì)

These characters are made up of two parts: one is a limited set of pictographs, often graphically simplified, which suggests the general meaning of the character, and the other is an existing character pronounced approximately as the new target word.

Examples:

hú	hé	liú
湖	河	流
lake	river	stream

All these characters above have on the left a radical of three short strokes, which is a simplified pictograph for a river, indicating that the character has a semantic connection with water. The right-hand side in each case is a phonetic indicator.

Due to the extremely productive use of this technique to extend the Chinese vocabulary, approximately 80% of characters fall into this category.

3 Strokes of Chinese characters

Chinese characters are formed by various kinds of strokes. Modern Chinese characters have six basic strokes.

	Stroke	Name	Meaning	Movement
❶	一	héng 横	horizontal stroke	left to right
❷	丨	shù 竖	vertical stroke	top to bottom
❸	丿	piě 撇	left-falling stroke	top right to bottom left
❹	㇏	nà 捺	right-falling stroke	top left to bottom right
❺	丶	diǎn 点	dot	top to bottom right
❻	㇀	tí 提	upward stroke	bottom left to top right

Apart from the six basic strokes, there are three dependent strokes: the bend (弯, wān), the turn (折, zhé), and the hook (钩, gōu). The dependent strokes cannot be used independently; they have to be attached to at least one other kind of stroke to form a complex stroke. The six basic strokes and the three dependent strokes together form all of the twenty-seven complex strokes used in modern Chinese characters.

The character 永 (yǒng, forever) below is a good example which combines most of the basic and dependent strokes.

4 Basic stroke order rules

❶ Strokes at the top should be written before those at the bottom.

三 三 三

❷ Strokes to the left should be written before those to the right.

八 八

❸ Horizontal strokes should be written before the vertical strokes or the left-falling strokes if they cross each other.

十 十

❹ Enclosing strokes should be written first, then the strokes in the enclosed, followed by the sealing horizontal stroke.

四 四 四 四 四

5 Radicals

Almost all Chinese characters contain a particular component called a "radical" or "side" (偏旁, piānpáng). Some of these components were once characters themselves, for example, 山 (mountain), 日 (sun), 月 (moon) and 木 (tree).

The radical is usually the semantic root of the character, and in some cases it may also serve as a phonetic indicator. Radicals are placed either on the left, right, top, bottom, or outside of a character. By understanding the radicals, it will be much easier to learn Chinese characters.

There are more than 200 radicals. Below is a short list of some common ones.

Radical	Name	Meaning	Examples		
❶ 氵	sāndiǎnshuǐ 三点水	water	江 (jiāng, river)	河 (hé, river)	湖 (hú, lake)
❷ 亻	dānrénpáng 单人旁	person	你 (nǐ, you)	他 (tā, he)	体 (tǐ, body)
❸ 扌	tíshǒupáng 提手旁	hand	打 (dǎ, hit)	抱 (bào, hug)	拎 (līn, carry)
❹ 忄	shùxīnpáng 竖心旁	heart	情 (qíng, feeling)	忧 (yōu, sad)	愤 (fèn, angry)
❺ 宀	bǎogàitóu 宝盖头	roof	家 (jiā, home)	宅 (zhái, house)	室 (shì, room)
❻ 艹	cǎozìtóu 草字头	grass	草 (cǎo, grass)	花 (huā, flower)	芽 (yá, sprout)

6 Simplified and traditional Chinese characters

In 1956 and 1964, the People's Republic of China, in an effort to make Chinese language learning easier and boost literacy rates, released a list of simplified Chinese characters. The simplification reduced the number of strokes of a set of Chinese characters in the regular script. This was the most intensive effort undertaken to simplify Chinese characters in many years.

Since then, simplified Chinese characters have been officially adopted for use in mainland China, while Hong Kong, Macau and Taiwan remained unaffected by the reform. Singapore underwent three rounds of character simplification, eventually arriving at the same set of simplified characters as mainland China after the final round in 1976.

(In this book, the Chinese text is printed in simplified characters with the corresponding traditional characters listed in New Words and at the end of each lesson in the section of "I have learned.")

Below is a famous saying by Confucius (c. 551 B.C. - 479 B.C). The characters that have been simplified are highlighted.

Xué ér shí xí zhī,   bú yì yuè hū?

Traditional form: 學而時習之，不亦說乎？

Simplified form: 学而时习之，不亦说乎？

(Learning and putting it into practice when the need arises — isn't that deeply satisfying?)

7 Chinese calligraphy

Calligraphy is not only a practical technique for writing Chinese characters, but also a unique oriental art of expression. In the past two thousand years, Chinese people have used ink brush to write on paper. The ink brush, ink, rice paper, and inkstone were essential implements of Chinese calligraphy, and they were known together as the Four Treasures of Study.

According to an old Chinese saying, "The way characters are written is a portrait of the person who writes them." Expressing the abstract beauty of lines and rhythms, calligraphy can be a reflection of a person's emotions, character and intellectual tastes. In ancient times, calligraphy was one of the Four Arts that scholars had to master.

Below is the most famous piece of Chinese calligraphy, *Preface to the Poems Composed at the Orchid Pavilion*. It was written by Wang Xizhi (303-361), the Sage of Calligraphy. The preface consisted of 324 Chinese characters in 28 lines. The character 之 (zhī) appears 17 times, but amazingly, none of them looks the same.

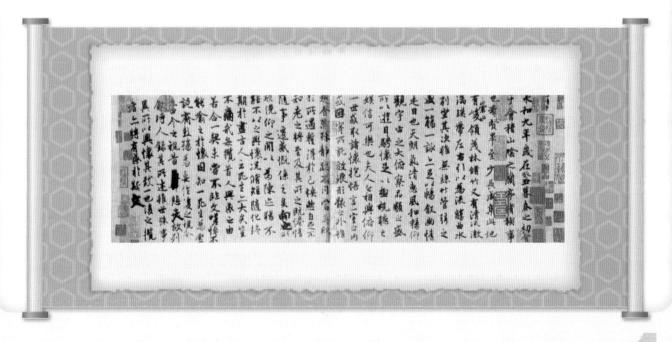

8 How to look up characters in a Chinese dictionary

There are two ways to look up words in a Chinese dictionary.

A. Using *pinyin*

1. Identify the *pinyin* of the character you wish to look up in the dictionary.
2. Following the usual alphabetical order as that in English dictionaries, and the order of the four tones, search for the entry in the dictionary.

B. Using radical and stroke count

1. Identify the radical of the character.
2. Count the number of strokes in the radical.
3. Find this radical and its page number from the Radical Index, which is categorized by the stroke count.
4. Turn to the page as found in Step 3, find the radical and then count the number of strokes in the character excluding the radical.
5. Find the character listed under the corresponding stroke count, then note its page number.
6. Turn to the page as found in Step 5 and find the entry.

1. Guess the meaning of the pictograms.

❶ 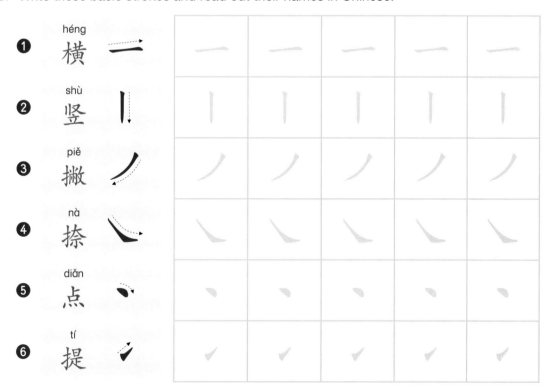 人   man, people

❷ _____

❸ _____

❹ _____

❺ _____

❻ _____

❼ _____

❽ _____

❾ _____

❿ _____

⓫ _____

⓬ _____

⓭ _____

⓮ _____

⓯ _____

⓰ _____

2. Circle the radicals of the characters.

❶ 海洋   ❷ 打扫   ❸ 冰冷   ❹ 芬芳

❺ 他们   ❻ 安宁   ❼ 说话   ❽ 热烈

3. Write these basic strokes and read out their names in Chinese.

❶ héng 横 ⟶	一	一	一	一	一	一
❷ shù 竖	丨	丨	丨	丨	丨	丨
❸ piě 撇	丿	丿	丿	丿	丿	丿
❹ nà 捺	乀	乀	乀	乀	乀	乀
❺ diǎn 点	丶	丶	丶	丶	丶	丶
❻ tí 提	✓	✓	✓	✓	✓	✓

4. Write these complex strokes, paying attention to the direction of the stroke movement as indicated.

❶	㇆	㇆	㇆	㇆	㇆	㇆
❷	㇆	㇆	㇆	㇆	㇆	㇆
❸	㇊	㇊	㇊	㇊	㇊	㇊
❹	㇄	㇄	㇄	㇄	㇄	㇄
❺	㇂	㇂	㇂	㇂	㇂	㇂
❻	乙	乙	乙	乙	乙	乙

5. Practice writing the following characters according to the stroke order shown.

四 四 四 四 四

sì 四 four	四	四			

五 五 五 五

wǔ 五 five	五	五			

六 六 六 六

liù 六 six	六	六			

九 九

| jiǔ
九
nine | 九 | 九 | | | |

你 你 你 你 你 你 你

| nǐ
你
you | 你 | 你 | | | |

我 我 我 我 我 我 我

| wǒ
我
I/me | 我 | 我 | | | |

他 他 他 他 他

| tā
他
he; him | 他 | 他 | | | |

是 是 是 是 是 是 是 是 是

| shì
是
verb "to be" | 是 | 是 | | | |

6. The top row of characters is in simplified form and the bottom row is in traditional form. Match them accordingly.

Nice to meet you!

你好!

COMMUNICATIVE GOALS

- Greeting people
- Introducing yourself and others
- Asking how people are
- Asking for someone's name and surname

Cultural Knowledge

- Greetings around the world
- Chinese words used in English
- The proper ways to greet different people
- Addressing a Chinese person
- Chinese names

Get ready...

1. Look at the pictures above showing how people in different countries greet each other. Can you guess which countries these people are from?

2. **Global Connection:** Do you know people around the world often borrow words from each other? You may already know some Chinese words that are used in English even before you start learning Chinese. Try to answer the following questions with your classmates.

   ◆ What Chinese words do you think you already know?
   ◆ What Chinese words are used in English?
   ◆ What Chinese people have you heard of?
   ◆ Do you have any friends or classmates who are Chinese?

Can you guess who I might be? What comes to mind when you first hear the word "Chinese"?

GREETING PEOPLE

A. Greeting one person
   你好! / 您好!

B. Greeting more than one person
   你们好! 同学们, 再见!

C. Greeting people you know
   叔叔, 您好!

MAKING INTRODUCTIONS

A. Telling one's name
   我是小伟。他是马丁。

B. Finding out who someone is
   他是谁? 他是王小伟。

STEP 3

ASKING HOW PEOPLE ARE

A. Asking and answering a greeting question
   你好吗? 我很好。

B. Going beyond general greetings
   你忙吗? 我很忙。

C. Replying in the negative
   我不忙。

ASKING SOMEONE'S NAME

A. Asking for someone's name
   你叫什么? 我叫李小成。

B. Asking for someone's surname
   你姓什么? 我姓张。

21

nǐ hǎo
你 好!
Hello!

你 好!

你 好!

A Greeting one person

你 好!　　您 好!
　　　　　nín

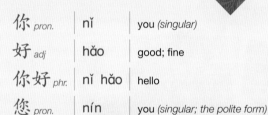

NEW WORDS
生词

你 pron.	nǐ	you (singular)
好 adj	hǎo	good; fine
你 好 phr.	nǐ hǎo	hello
您 pron.	nín	you (singular; the polite form)

LANGUAGE FOCUS

"你好!" is the most common greeting in Chinese. It can be used to greet people when you first meet them or to greet people you already know. It is appropriate for any time of the day.

When you meet people of the older generation or important people, for example, teachers, use the polite form 您 instead of 你 to show respect.

There are many other ways of greeting. For example, some young people greet each other using the word 嗨 (hāi). It probably originated from the English language.

1. Greet your teacher and classmates using 你好 or 您好.

2. Would you use 你好 or 您好 to greet the following people?

1 A classmate

2 The school principal

3 Your Chinese teacher

4 The doctor in a hospital

5 Your friend

6 Your friend's father

7 Your friend's mother

8 Your grandfather

DO YOU KNOW . . .
你知道吗?

Sometimes, to greet someone on different occasions, you may also try these common expressions:

ma
➤ 你 好 吗 ?
How are you?

shàngwǔ   zǎo
➤ 上 午 好 ! / 你 早 ! / 早 !
Good morning!   Good morning!   Good morning!

xiàwǔ   wǎnshang
➤ 下 午 好 ! / 晚 上 好 !
Good afternoon!   Good evening!

nǐmen
你们好!
Hello!

lǎoshī
老师好!
Hello, Ms. Smith (name of the teacher)!

tóngxuémen
同学们好!
Hello, class!

zàijiàn
同学们，再见!
Goodbye, class!

老师，再见!
Goodbye, Mr Johnson!

生 词

NEW WORDS

你们 pron.	你們	nǐmen	you (plural)
老师 n.	老師	lǎoshī	teacher
同学 n.	同學	tóngxué	classmate
再见 v.	再見	zàijiàn	see you again; goodbye

LANGUAGE FOCUS

The word 们 can be used to change singular nouns or pronouns about people into plural forms. For example, 你 (singular) together with 们 becomes 你们 (plural) and it refers to "you," meaning more than one person.

"同学们" is a common expression used by teachers to address a group of students.

Putting 同学 with 们 changes the word to the plural form.

When you say 再见 to someone, use the same pattern as you did for 你好. You can simply say 再见 to someone, which literally means "see again." You may also add the addressee in front, such as "王老师，再见！" or "同学们，再见！"

1. Imagine you are saying "hello" in Chinese. Match the English descriptions to the Chinese greetings listed below, and read the correct Chinese greetings aloud.

   How would you say "hello" in Chinese when you greet . . .

   1 a young person   你们好!

   2 a teacher   您好!

   3 a group of people   你好!

   4 an elderly person   同学们好!

   5 your classmates   老师好!

2. Now imagine you are saying "goodbye" in Chinese. Match the English descriptions to the Chinese leave-taking statements. Read the correct Chinese greetings aloud.

   How would you say "goodbye" in Chinese to . . .

   1 your friend's father   Mǎkè (马克)，再见!

   2 your teacher   同学们，再见!

   3 Mark   shūshu (叔叔)，再见!

   4 a group of students   Ānqí (安琪)，再见!

   5 Angie   老师，再见!

In typical Chinese classrooms, when the teacher walks into the class, students stand up to exchange greetings with the teacher. Sometimes students and teachers also bow to each other to show mutual respect.

老师：同学们好!

同学：老师好!

bàba　　māma

爸爸、妈妈，你们好！

Hi, Dad and Mom!

shūshu

叔叔，您好！

Hi, Uncle!

āyí

阿姨，您好！

Hi, Auntie!

NEW WORDS 生词

爸爸 n.	bàba		father
妈妈 n.	媽媽	māma	mother
叔叔 n.	shūshu		uncle
阿姨 n.	āyí		aunt, auntie
王 p.n.	Wáng		(a common Chinese surname)
李 p.n.	Lǐ		(a common Chinese surname)
张 p.n.	張	Zhāng	(a common Chinese surname)

LANGUAGE FOCUS

When greeting a person you know, you may say the person's name or title first followed by 你好 or 您好. When talking to a friend's parents, Chinese children will often address them as 叔叔 or 阿姨, normally adding their last names in front.

Examples:

Lǐ

李老师，您好！

Hi, Miss Li!

Wáng

王叔叔，您好！

Hi, Uncle Wang!

Try This!

1. Say "hello" in Chinese to the following people using their name or title.

❶ 王老师，您好！

❷ Mǎkè (马克)

❸ Ānqí (安琪)

❹ 李叔叔

❺ 张阿姨

❻ Uncle John

2. Now say "goodbye" to the same people above using 再见.

叔叔，再见！

DO YOU KNOW ...
你知道吗?

Do you know that in many countries, the way to pronounce the words for "mother" and "father" sounds very similar across languages? Americans, Chinese, Germans, and Iranians (as well as people of many other languages) all call their parents using similar sounding words like "mama" and "papa."

Papa!

To find out more, use the Internet and search for the words for "mother" and "father" in different languages and compare them.

NEW WORDS

我 *pron.*	wǒ	I; me
他 *pron.*	tā	he; him
她 *pron.*	tā	she; her
是 *v.*	shì	am, is, are *(verb "to be")*
叫 *v.*	jiào	call, be called

A Telling one's name

wǒ shì   Xiǎowěi
我 是 王 小 伟。
I am Wang Xiaowei.

tā   Mǎdīng
他 是 马 丁。
He is Martin.

tā jiào   Fāngfang
她 叫 李 芳 芳。
She is called Li Fangfang.

LANGUAGE FOCUS

When you tell people your name, use 是. It is similar to the verbs "to be" (is, am, are) in English. In Chinese the verb 是 does not change form no matter who the subject is.

It is also very common to introduce one's name in this pattern:

我叫王小伟。他叫……，她叫……。

CULTURAL HIGHLIGHTS

Chinese Names

All Chinese people have a name which usually includes a surname 姓 (xìng) and a given name 名 (míng). Given names may consist of one or two characters and are written after the family or surname. For example, for the Chinese name 王小伟, the surname is 王 and the given name is 小伟.

The surname and given name of Chinese people should be written separately when using *pinyin* to spell the name, and the first letter of both the surname and the given name should be capitalized, for example, Wang Xiaowei.

One interesting point to note is that in Chinese names, the surname is placed before the given name. This is different from English names, where the last name (surname) is placed after the first name (given name).

1. Greet your classmate sitting next to you by saying 你好 first, and then tell your name. Turn to other classmates to say hello and tell your name.

2. Work with a partner. Take turns to introduce the persons in the photo and greet them. Challenge yourself by pronouncing their Chinese names. You've already come across all these characters!

Student A: 他是马丁。   Student B: 马丁，你好！

王安   丁小同

张芳   马琪   李伟

shéi

她 是 谁 ？
Who is she?

她 是 李 老 师 。
She is Miss Li.

他 是 谁 ？
Who is he?

他 是 王 小 伟 。
He is Wang Xiaowei.

生 词

NEW WORD

谁 *pron.* | 誰 | shéi, shuí | who

LANGUAGE FOCUS

To find out who someone is, ask the question "他是谁?" The reply could be a term of address for the person, e.g. "她是李老师。", or the person's name, e.g. "他是王小伟。"

Examples:	Questions	Answers
❶	你 是 谁 ？ Who are you?	我 是 李 芳 芳 。 I am Li Fangfang.
❷	她 是 谁 ？ Who is she?	她 是 张 阿 姨 。 She is Auntie Zhang.

Try This!

1. Referring to the pictures below, work with a classmate by asking and answering the question "他 (她) 是谁?". Respond using the sentence pattern "他 (她) 是……" and the names provided.

Wáng Xiǎowěi
❶ 王小伟

Lǐ Fāngfang
❷ 李芳芳

Mǎdīng
❸ 马丁

Zhāng Ānqí
❹ 张安琪

Lǐ lǎoshī
❺ 李老师

2. Bring in pictures of your friends or family members and introduce them to your classmates by telling their names.

他是谁?

ASKING HOW PEOPLE ARE

ma
你好吗?
How are you?

hěn   xièxie
我很好，谢谢!
I'm fine.   Thank you!

A Asking and answering a greeting question

你好吗?
How are you?

hái   kěyǐ
还可以。
I'm okay.

NEW WORDS

吗 part.	嗎	ma	(a question word)
很好 phr.	很好	hěn hǎo	fine
谢谢 v.	謝謝	xièxie	thank you
还可以 phr.	還可以	hái kěyǐ	okay; not bad

LANGUAGE FOCUS

People who already know each other often greet each other with "你好吗?" (*How are you?*) The word 吗 in Chinese is used to ask a question. The common reply is, "我很好。" (*I'm fine.*)

Note that in this context 很 does not mean "very," so it does not intensify the degree of the adjective following it.

After replying with 我很好, sometimes people add 谢谢 (*thank you*) to be polite.

If you think things are not going too badly, you may reply with another expression "还可以" to indicate that things are okay.

When the question marker 吗 is attached to the end of a statement, a question is formed. For example:

Statement: 他是马丁。   Question: 他是马丁吗?

To create a question in English, you often put the verb "do" or a form of the verb "to be" in front of the statement. In Chinese, the question is formed by retaining the word order and adding 吗 at the end.

1. Say "hello" to three classmates and ask how they are doing. Use the following sample dialog as a model.

      hāi

Ⓐ 嗨！芳芳！   Ⓐ 芳芳，你好吗?

     Ⓑ 嗨！小伟！   Ⓑ 我很好，谢谢！

2. Change the following sentences into questions using 吗:

❶ 你好。   ❺ 他是老师。

❷ 她是张阿姨。   ❻ 他是王叔叔。

❸ 她是你朋友 (péngyou, friend)。   ❼ 她是张芳 (Zhāng Fāng)。

❹ 你是玛丽 (Mǎlì, Mary)。   ❽ 他是马丁 (Mǎdīng, Martin)。

máng

你 忙 吗？
Are you busy?

我 很 忙。
Yes, I am.

生 词

NEW WORDS

忙 *adj.*	máng	busy
累 *adj.*	lèi	tired

lèi

你 累 吗？
Are you tired?

我 很 累。
Yes, I am.

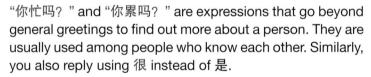

LANGUAGE FOCUS

"你忙吗？" and "你累吗？" are expressions that go beyond general greetings to find out more about a person. They are usually used among people who know each other. Similarly, you also reply using 很 instead of 是.

For example: 我很忙。我很累。

Answer the following questions:

❶ 你们忙吗？

❷ 你累吗？ ⟶ 我很累。

❸ 她爸爸忙吗？

❹ 芳芳好吗？

❺ 老师忙吗？

❻ 你忙吗？

你忙吗?
Are you busy?

bù
我不忙。
No, I'm not.

bú
你累吗? 我不累。
Are you tired?   No, I'm not.

生 词

NEW WORD

不 *adv.* | bù | not

LANGUAGE FOCUS

To negate a sentence in Chinese, place the word 不 before the adjective or the verb. Look at more examples below:

Questions

❶ 妈 妈 忙 吗 ?
Is Mom busy?

❷ 您 是 王 老 师 吗 ?
Are you Miss Wang?

Answers

妈 妈 不 忙 。
No, she's not.

我 不 是 王 老 师 。
No, I'm not.

THE TONE FOR 不

The tone for 不 changes in some instances. It stays as a fourth tone if it is followed by a first, second, or a third tone word, e.g., bù máng (不忙), bù hǎo (不好). But 不 changes to the second tone bú when it is followed by a word in the fourth tone, e.g., bú shì (不是), bú lèi (不累).

❶
你 累 吗？
bú lèi
我 不 累 。

❷
你 们 忙 吗？
bù máng
我 们 不 忙 。

Try This!

1. Negate the following sentences by using 不:

   ❶ 他是老师。 ⟶ 他不是老师。　❹ 她是李阿姨。

   ❷ 我是马丁。　❺ 我们是同学。

   ❸ 她是芳芳。　❻ 他是张叔叔。

2. Work with a classmate to ask the following questions and answer in the negative:

   ❶ 爸爸，您累吗？　❹ 你是小伟吗？

   ❷ 您是老师吗？　❺ 她是李阿姨吗？

   ❸ 他妈妈忙吗？　❻ 叔叔，您忙吗？

3. Work in a group of three. One student is to greet the others in the question format with 吗, and the others are to reply either in the affirmative or in the negative.

shénme   míngzi

你 叫 什么 名字？

What is your name?

Xiǎochéng.

我 叫 李 小 成。

My name is Li Xiaocheng.

A Asking for someone's name

你 叫 什么？

What's your name?

Luóbótè.

我 叫 罗 伯 特。

My name is Robert.

LANGUAGE FOCUS

You can add 什么 to a declarative statement to form a question. To ask a person's name, say: "你叫什么名字?". Colloquially, people simply ask "你叫什么?", which literally means: *You call yourself what?* In reply, people may give their first or given name or answer with their full name.

生 词

NEW WORDS

| 什么 pron. | 什麼 | shénme | what |
| 名字 n. | | míngzi | name |

 CULTURAL HIGHLIGHTS

Addressing a Chinese Person

When Chinese people first meet, they seldom call others directly by their given names. Instead, they address people by their surnames followed by a title that indicates their position or profession. For example, 王先生 (Wáng xiānsheng, Mr. Wang) and 张老师 (Zhāng lǎoshī, *lit.* Teacher Zhang).

Given names are usually used among friends and family members. At schools in China, teachers often call students by their full names, and students also call each other by full names.

1. Figure out how the following English names are pronounced in Chinese and match them with the correct *pinyin* spellings. The Chinese characters are provided in brackets.

❶ Mary   Luóbótè （罗伯特）   ❺ Lucy   Àidéhuá （爱德华）

❷ Carolyn   Mǎlì   （玛丽）   ❻ Anna   Lǐchádé （理查德）

❸ James   Zhānmǔsī （詹姆斯）   ❼ Richard   Ānnà   （安娜）

❹ Robert   Kǎluòlín （卡洛琳）   ❽ Edward   Lùxī   （露西）

2. Look at the following pictures and ask a classmate "他/她叫什么名字?" Then have that student answer the question.

他叫孔子。

3. Bring in five pictures of famous people found on the Internet or in a magazine and practice asking "他/她叫什么?" Call on other students to answer your question.

xìng

你 姓 什么？
What's your surname?

我 姓 李。
My surname is Li.

LANGUAGE FOCUS

In China, people often ask what your surname is, especially when you first meet someone. 姓 is used as a verb (it means "to be surnamed") in asking and answering questions about a person's surname. When you ask for another person's surname, use the following pattern:

❶ 你 姓 什么？
   我 姓 张。

❷ 他 姓 什么？
   他 姓 李。

When asking for the surname of an important person, a person of the older generation, a person holding a senior position, or a person they first meet, most Chinese would apply the following to show respect:

❸ 您 贵 姓？
   我 姓 王。

guì

您 贵 姓？
What's your surname?

我 姓 王。
My surname is Wang.

NEW WORDS

姓 v./n.	xìng	be surnamed; surname
贵姓 phr. 贵姓	guìxìng	(used to ask for one's surname in a polite way)

1. Introduce yourself to your classmates. Go around the room and see how many classmates you can meet and introduce yourself to in two minutes. Ask your teacher's name and tell him/her your name.

2. Find a picture of yourself and write underneath it in Chinese what your name is (我是…… or 我叫……, 我姓……). Place a copy of your picture in your portfolio.

3. Give a Chinese name to your parents and family members.

 CULTURAL HIGHLIGHTS

Choosing a Chinese Name

Here is a list of Chinese characters to help you choose your Chinese name. You may wish to have a full Chinese name with a surname and a given name, or simply a Chinese given name in one or two characters. Your teacher will help you decide. The given names are listed with English translations. You may also look up on the Internet to choose other names.

Ten Most Common Chinese Surnames

1. 李 Lǐ   2. 王 Wáng   3. 张 Zhāng   4. 刘 Liú   5. 陈 Chén

6. 杨 Yáng   7. 赵 Zhào   8. 黄 Huáng   9. 周 Zhōu   10. 吴 Wú

Popular Words for Male Given Names

1. 伟 wěi   great, big
2. 明 míng   bright
3. 刚 gāng   hard, solid, unyielding, firm

4. 强 qiáng   strong
5. 平 píng   peaceful, smooth
6. 杰 jié   outstanding

Popular Words for Female Given Names

1. 芳 fāng   fragrant
2. 艳 yàn   colorful
3. 丽 lì   beautiful

4. 娜 nà   beautiful
5. 静 jìng   tranquil, quiet
6. 娟 juān   beautiful, graceful

DIALOG *in Context*

STEP 1
GREETING PEOPLE

Greeting a teacher

王老师，您好！
　　小伟，你好！

Greeting a principal "Good morning!"

李校长，您早！
　　你们早！

Greeting neighbors

叔叔好！阿姨好！
　　安琪，你好！
　　　　安琪，上午好！
叔叔、阿姨，再见！

STEP 2
MAKING INTRODUCTIONS

Introducing yourself to the class

你好！我是张芳。
　　你好！我叫小伟。
他是谁？
　　他是马克。
她是谁？
　　她是王老师。
谢谢！

STEP 3
ASKING HOW PEOPLE ARE

Exchanging greetings amongst friends

嗨，安琪，你好吗？
　　我很好。
小伟，你好吗？
　　还可以，谢谢！

Asking parents how they are
(to show concern)

妈妈，你忙吗？
　　我很忙。
爸爸，你累吗？
　　我不累，你妈妈很累。

STEP 4
ASKING SOMEONE'S NAME

Exchanging greetings with an adult

叔叔，您好！
　　你好！你叫什么名字？
我叫小伟。
　　你姓什么？
我姓王。您贵姓？
　　我姓张。她是谁？
她是我同学，她叫安琪。
　　安琪，你好！
　　　　张叔叔，您好！
　　你们忙吗？
我们不忙。张叔叔，再见！
　　再见！

Step Up!

1. **Introduce** yourself and others. Divide into groups of three.

   ◆ Student A says hello to the other two students first, and then introduces himself/herself.
   ◆ Student B then introduces himself/herself to the group and introduces Student A and C.
   ◆ Repeat the activity by switching roles until every student has introduced himself/herself and also has been introduced.
   ◆ Then form different groups of three and repeat the same introductions.

2. **Write** a short introduction about yourself (*saying hello and stating your name*) and put it in your portfolio. You may write in *pinyin* or challenge yourself with some writing in characters. *For example*, 你们好，我是马丁。

3. **Create** an electronic portfolio to show how well you can use the Chinese words you have learned in this lesson. Make a home page with a picture of yourself. Write a caption or insert speech bubbles to greet and introduce yourself to the viewers of your portfolio.

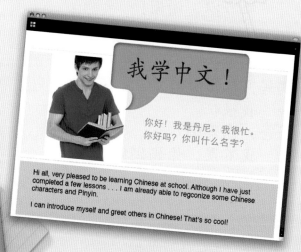

Fun Time!

Chanting in Chinese makes learning easy and fun. You may use cheers, chants, raps, songs, and poetry to practice and use new vocabulary. You may read aloud with classmates or follow your teacher to repeat the following rhymes.

1

Nǐ hǎo,   nǐ hǎo,   nǐ hǎo ma?
你 好 ， 你 好 ， 你 好 吗 ？

Hěn hǎo,   hěn hǎo,   wǒ hěn hǎo.
很 好 ， 很 好 ， 我 很 好 。

2

Wǒ wǒ wǒ,   nǐ nǐ nǐ,
我 我 我 ， 你 你 你 ，

Wǒ hé nǐ,   nǐ hé wǒ,
我 和 你 ， 你 和 我 ，
(and)

Wǒmen   dōu shì hǎo péngyou.
我 们 都 是 好 朋 友 。
(All of us are good friends.)

3

Xièxie,   xièxie,   xièxie nǐ!
谢 谢 ， 谢 谢 ， 谢 谢 你 ！

Bú xiè,   bú xiè,   búyòng xiè.
不 谢 ， 不 谢 ， 不 用 谢 。
(Don't mention it.)

I have learned...

Core Vocabulary

你 pron.		nǐ	you (singular)	是 v.		shì	am, is, are (verb "to be")
您 pron.		nín	you (singular; the polite form)	谁 pron.	誰	shéi, shuí	who
好 adj.		hǎo	good; fine	吗 part.	嗎	ma	(a question word)
你好 phr.		nǐ hǎo	hello	很好 phr.		hěn hǎo	fine
我 pron.		wǒ	I; me	不 adv.		bù	not
他 pron.		tā	he; him	叫 v.		jiào	call; be called
她 pron.		tā	she; her	什么 pron.	什麼	shénme	what
你们 pron.	你們	nǐmen	you (plural)	姓 v. / n.		xìng	be surnamed; surname

Extended Vocabulary

再见 v.	再見	zàijiàn	see you again; goodbye	嗨 interj.		hāi	hi
谢谢 v.	謝謝	xièxie	thank you	你早 phr.		nǐ zǎo	good morning
名字 n.		míngzi	name	上午 n.		shàngwǔ	morning
老师 n.	老師	lǎoshī	teacher	下午 n.		xiàwǔ	afternoon
同学 n.	同學	tóngxué	classmate	晚上 n.		wǎnshang	evening
爸爸 n.		bàba	father	还可以 phr.	還可以	hái kěyǐ	okay; not bad
妈妈 n.	媽媽	māma	mother	忙 adj.		máng	busy
叔叔 n.		shūshu	uncle	累 adj.		lèi	tired
阿姨 n.		āyí	aunt, auntie	贵姓 phr.	貴姓	guìxìng	(used to ask for one's surname in a polite way)

Proper Nouns

Common Chinese Surnames	张 張 Zhāng	王 Wáng	李 Lǐ	
Other Names (Step 2 and 4)	小伟 小偉 Xiǎowěi	芳芳 Fāngfang	马丁 馬丁 Mǎdīng	
	罗伯特 羅伯特 Luóbótè	小成 Xiǎochéng	马克 馬克 Mǎkè	

SENTENCE PATTERNS

你好! / 您好!	你好吗? 我很好，谢谢! / 还可以。
你们好! / 同学们好!	你忙吗? 我很忙。 / 我不忙。
老师，您好! / 爸爸，您好! / 妈妈，您好!	你叫什么名字? / 你叫什么?
王叔叔、李阿姨，你们好!	我叫李小成。
再见!	你姓什么? 我姓王。
我是小伟。她是芳芳。他是马丁。	您贵姓? 我姓张。
你是谁? 我是芳芳。	

I can do!

Interpretive Communication

❑ I can understand when someone is greeting me.

❑ I can understand when someone asks me how I am.

❑ I can understand when someone tells me that he/she is well or busy.

❑ I can understand when someone asks for my name and surname.

❑ I can read a common greeting in Chinese.

❑ I can read some characters in *pinyin*.

Interpersonal Communication

❑ I can exchange greetings with someone or with a group of people.

❑ I can greet different people using the appropriate pronoun.

❑ I can exchange information on my name with someone.

❑ I can ask and answer very simple questions.

❑ I can exchange words to express courtesy.

❑ I can exchange a farewell with someone or with a group of people.

Presentational Communication

❑ I can tell people who I am by stating my name.

❑ I can introduce my parents to others.

❑ I can introduce a friend to others.

❑ I can tell people that I am well or busy.

❑ I can state some sentences in the negative.

Cultural Knowledge

❑ I can use culturally appropriate ways to greet people.

❑ I can describe how the teacher and students greet each other in a Chinese classroom.

❑ I can identify the surname and given name in Chinese.

❑ I can compare names in English and Chinese.

❑ I can ask for a person's surname.

❑ I can address a Chinese person in an appropriate way.

LESSON 2

Getting to know you

你是哪国人?

COMMUNICATIVE GOALS

* Asking and telling one's nationality
* Discussing one's hometown
* Asking and telling where one lives

Cultural Knowledge

* The Chinese concept of hometown
* Beijing and Shanghai
* Celebrities from China and other countries
* Features of a Chinese ID card

Get ready...

Before you begin to learn how to ask in Chinese simple questions such as "Where are you from?", or "What is your nationality?", it will be helpful to first get acquainted with the Chinese names of some of the countries listed below. Then, locate these countries on a world map.

Australia
Àodàlìyà
澳大利亚

Brazil
Bāxī
巴西

China
Zhōngguó
中国

France
Fǎguó
法国

U.K.
Yīngguó
英国

Germany
Déguó
德国

India
Yìndù
印度

Japan
Rìběn
日本

Mexico
Mòxīgē
墨西哥

South Africa
Nánfēi
南非

Spain
Xībānyá
西班牙

U.S.A.
Měiguó
美国

*T*hink about what you would say to a classmate from a different country after saying "Hi!" . . .

STEPS *at a glance!*

STEP 1

ABOUT ONE'S NATIONALITY

A. Asking one's nationality
你是哪国人？我是中国人。

B. Asking yes-no questions about one's nationality
你是美国人吗？
对，我是美国人。

C. Asking about the nationality of a third person
她也是美国人吗？
对，我们都是美国人。

STEP 2

ABOUT ONE'S HOMETOWN
你是哪里人？我是北京人。

STEP 3

ABOUT WHERE ONE LIVES

A. Asking where one's home is
你家在哪儿？我家在北京。

B. Specifying directions
你家在哪里？我家在西边。

C. Asking where one lives
你住哪儿？我住这儿。

49

nǎ guó rén
你 是 哪 国 人?
Which country are you from?

Měiguórén
我 是 美 国 人。
I am American.

| Name | Caroline P. Andrews | Nationality | 美国 |
| Gender | 女 | Age | 14 |

A Asking one's nationality

| Name | 李伟 | Nationality | 中国 |
| Gender | 男 | Age | 13 |

他 是 哪 国 人?
What is his nationality?

zhōng
他 是 中 国 人。
He is Chinese.

生 词 NEW WORDS

哪 *pron.*	nǎ	where; which				
国 *n.*	國	guó	country			
人 *n.*		rén	person; people	美国人 *n.*	美國人	Měiguórén	American
男 *n.*		nán	male	中国人 *n.*	中國人	Zhōngguórén	Chinese
女 *n.*		nǚ	female				

LANGUAGE FOCUS

"你是哪国人?" is a question used to find out someone's nationality. It literally means "You are a person from which country?"

Examples:

David 是哪国人?　What is David's nationality?

她是哪国人?　What is her nationality?

To state your nationality, combine the country name with 人.

Examples:

美国人 American 　　中国人 Chinese

yīng
英国人 British / English

fǎ
法国人 French

Try This!

1. Work with a classmate and take turns asking and answering questions about the nationalities of the people below. Follow the sample speech pattern provided. You may refer to Get Ready for the names of different countries.

> Student A: 他／她叫什么？他／她是哪国人？
>
> Student B: 她叫Nicole。她是澳大利亚人。

Nicole
Australia

Lewis
Great Britain

Michelle
U.S.A.

Rafael
Spain

Miyagi
Japan

Zhang Ming
China

Angela
Germany

Nelson
South Africa

2. Ask at least five classmates about their parents' nationalities. Complete the chart in *pinyin*. If a parent comes from a country that has not been introduced to you, ask your teacher how to say it and share it with your classmates.

名字	妈妈是哪国人？	爸爸是哪国人？

你是中国人吗?
Are you Chinese?

duì
对，我是中国人。
Yes, I'm Chinese.

NEW WORDS

对 adj.	對	duì	yes; right
不是 phr.		bú shì	no
法国人 n.	法國人	Fǎguórén	French
英国人 n.	英國人	Yīngguórén	British; English

fǎ
她是法国人吗?
Is she French?

bú shì   yīng
不是，她是英国人。
No, she's British.

LANGUAGE FOCUS

When the question marker 吗 is attached to the end of a declarative sentence, a yes-no question (or interrogative sentence) is formed. If the answer to the question is positive, you can say 是 or 对 (*which means what you say is correct*). However, if the answer is negative, use 不 or 不是 (*which means what you say is not correct*). For negative answers, we usually add a corrective statement at the end:

他是美国人吗?

不，他不是美国人，他是英国人。

1. Ask the classmates around you about their nationalities. Pose a yes-no question and let them answer accordingly. Use the speech pattern you have learned in this section:

Student A: 你是……吗？   Student B: 对，我是……。/ 不是，我是……。

2. Work with a classmate to ask and answer questions about the nationalities of people in the pictures shown below. Use the nationalities provided for pictures 1 to 4 and practice the speech pattern shown in the box below. The answer should be a positive one.

Student A: 他是……人吗？   Student B: 对，他是……人。

❶ 中国人   ❷ 美国人   ❸ 法国人   ❹ 英国人

Next, for pictures 5 and 6, practice the speech pattern shown in the box below. The answer should be a negative one.

Student A: 她是……人吗？   Student B: 不是，她是……人。

❺ 中国人；日本人
　　　　　Rìběn   ❻ 英国人；法国人

你是哪国人?

① 我是美国人。

NEW WORDS 生 词

也 adv.	yě	also
都 adv.	dōu	both; all

yě
他也是美国人吗?
Is he American too?

dōu
② 对，我们都是美国人。
Yes. Both of us are Americans.

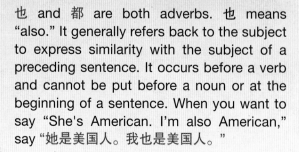

LANGUAGE FOCUS

也 and 都 are both adverbs. 也 means "also." It generally refers back to the subject to express similarity with the subject of a preceding sentence. It occurs before a verb and cannot be put before a noun or at the beginning of a sentence. When you want to say "She's American. I'm also American," say "她是美国人。我也是美国人。"

都, meaning "both/all," indicates inclusiveness. It is often used to sum up preceding elements. As with the word 也, it can only be put before a verb. When you want to say "We're all Chinese," say "我们都是中国人。"

1. Complete the following sentences.

❶ A: 我是英国人。

   B: 我＿＿＿是英国人。

   A: 我们＿＿＿是英国人。

❷ A: 我是法国人。你们是哪国人？

   B: 我们＿＿＿是中国人。

❸ A: 你是＿＿＿国人？

   B: 我是＿＿＿国人。

   A: 她＿＿＿是＿＿＿国人吗？

   B: 对，我们＿＿＿是＿＿＿国人。

❹ A: 他是法国人吗？

   B: ＿＿＿，他是法国人。

   A: 你＿＿＿是法国人吗？

   B: 对，我们＿＿＿是法国人。

2. Look at each pair of famous people, and make two simple sentences about their nationalities using 也 and 都. Apply the speech pattern shown in the box:

> 1. (Person A) 是……，(Person B) 也是……。
>
> 2. 他们都是……。

❶

China

Láng Lǎng
郎 朗

Zhāng Zǐyí
章子怡

❷

U.K.

J.K. Rowling

Prince William

nǎlǐ
你是哪里人？
Where are you from?

Běijīng
我是北京人。
I'm from Beijing.

NEW WORDS

生词

哪里 pron.	哪裏	nǎlǐ	where
北京 n.	Běijīng		Beijing
上海 n.	Shànghǎi		Shanghai
香港 n.	Xiānggǎng		Hong Kong
西安 n.	Xī'ān		Xi'an

你是哪里人？
Where are you from?

Shànghǎi
我是上海人。
I'm from Shanghai.

LANGUAGE FOCUS

"你是哪里人？" is often used for asking about one's hometown when Chinese people first meet. The concept of hometown is very important to Chinese, as it not only stands for the native place of someone or his ancestors, but also tells about one's cultural roots, dialect group, the type of cuisine one is accustomed to, and much more. For people who work or travel far from their hometowns, they will feel the natural and cultural bond when they meet someone from their hometown.

1. Pictures 1 through 4 show the hometowns of four individuals. Practice asking and saying the sample speech below about the hometown where each individual is from.

Student A: 张小伟是哪里人？   Student B: 他是……人。

张小伟   北京   陈芳芳   上海   李小成   香港   张美英   西安

2. **Challenge Yourself:** Look at pictures 1 to 8. Can you guess which famous person, scene or food comes from Beijing, and which from Shanghai? Write the corresponding numbers in the boxes below. You may research online if you are not sure.

Next, practice by saying the hometowns of the two famous persons in pictures 6 and 8.

北京：☐ ☐ ☐ ☐

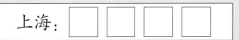

上海：☐ ☐ ☐ ☐

Oriental Pearl Tower
(Dōngfāng Míngzhūtǎ)

Peking Duck
(Běijīng Kǎoyā)

Steamed Pork Dumplings
(Xiǎo Lóng Bāo)

The Great Wall
(Cháng Chéng)

The Forbidden City
(Gù Gōng)

Last Emperor Puyi

The Bund
(Wàitān)

Yao Ming

jiā zài nǎr
你 家 在 哪 儿?
Where is your home?

我 家 在 北 京。
My home is in Beijing.

她 家 在 哪 里?
Where is her home?

zhèr
她 家 在 这 儿。
Her home is over here.

nàr
我 家 在 那 儿。
My home is over there.

A | Asking where one's home is

NEW WORDS 生词

家 ¹ n.	jiā	home
在 v.	zài	at
哪儿 pron.	哪兒 nǎr	where
这儿 pron.	這兒 zhèr	here
那儿 pron.	那兒 nàr	there

¹ another meaning also appears in Lesson 5

LANGUAGE FOCUS

"你家在哪儿？" or "你家在哪里？" are questions asking where one lives, or more specifically, where someone's home is. To reply, you either give a general location or a place name.

Examples: 我家在那儿。 My home is over there.
她家在上海。 Her home is in Shanghai.

哪里 and 哪儿 both mean "where." In China, people in the north usually say 哪儿, while people in the south say 哪里.

Challenge Yourself: Based on the *pinyin* and Chinese characters provided in the pictures, practice saying the dialog shown below. Next, match each picture to the correct English name by writing its corresponding number in the box next to the name.

1. 你家在哪儿？   2. 我家在北京。

Běijīng 北京

Shànghǎi 上海

Xiānggǎng 香港

☐ Shanghai   ☐ Hongkong   1 Beijing

Xī'ān 西安

Huáshèngdùn 华盛顿

Niǔyuē 纽约

☐ Washington, D.C.   ☐ Xi'an   ☐ New York

Zhījiāgē 芝加哥

Luòshānjī 洛杉矶

Bālí 巴黎

☐ Los Angeles   ☐ Chicago   ☐ Paris

Lúndūn 伦敦

Mòxīgē 墨西哥

Xīní 悉尼

☐ Sydney   ☐ Mexico   ☐ London

你家在哪里?
Where is your home?

xībian

我家在西边。 ←---------- 西
My home is in the West.

北

N

NW   NE

W   E 东

SW   SE

S

南

NEW WORDS

东 n.	東	dōng	east
南 n.		nán	south
西 n.		xī	west
北 n.		běi	north
边 n.	邊	biān	side

LANGUAGE FOCUS

It is also common to answer questions about where one lives by stating a direction—North (北), South (南), East (东) or West (西). In other words, if you know the direction, use the pattern "在 + directional word + 边" to tell where someone lives.

Try This!

1. Answer the following questions in Chinese. Follow the example.

   ❶ Which direction is New York from San Francisco? ___东边___

   ❷ Which direction is Shanghai from Beijing? _____

   ❸ Which direction is Norway from Finland? _____

   ❹ Which direction is America from Brazil? _____

   ❺ Which direction is London from Hong Kong? _____

2. Work with a classmate to ask and answer questions on where each of you lives. Follow the pattern.

   A: 你家在哪儿?   B: 我家在南边。

zhù

你 住 哪 儿?

Where do you live?

我 住 那 儿。

I live there.

她 住 哪 儿?

Where does she live?

她 住 东 边。

She lives in the East.

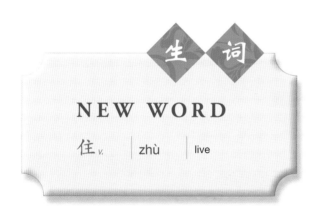

生 词

NEW WORD

| 住 v. | zhù | live |

LANGUAGE FOCUS

To ask where a person lives, say "住哪儿?" To answer, either provide an address or you could say "住那儿／这儿." This form of answer also gives an impression of "in that / this vicinity."

1. On the ID card shown below, pick out the correct answers to the questions found in the speech pattern box. Next, practice saying the questions and answers.

姓名: 王丽丽
性别: 女
国籍: 中国
出生日期: 1988年6月10日
住址: 中国北京市西城区
二龙路168号

公民身份号码: 010579198806104628

她叫什么?　　她叫……。

她是哪国人?　她是……人。

她是哪里人?　她是……人。

她住哪儿?　　她住……。

2. **Pair Work:** Practice saying specific directions in Chinese. Ask and say the directions of these places by applying this speech pattern:

Student A: 你住哪儿?　　　Student B: 我住……。

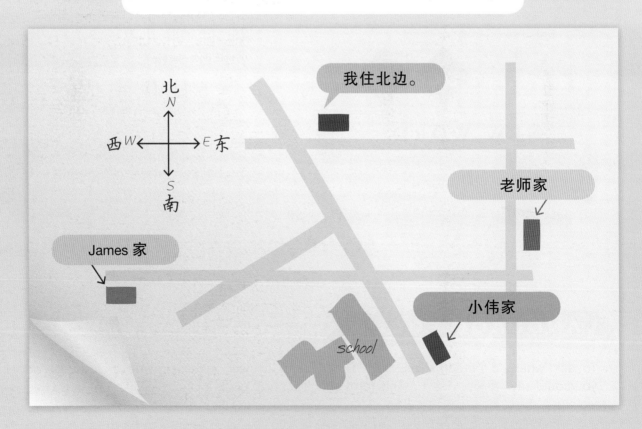

DIALOG *in* Context

STEP 1
ABOUT ONE'S NATIONALITY

Students introducing each other when meeting for the first time

你好！你叫什么名字？

　　我叫 Jacques。

你是法国人吗？

　　不是，我是美国人。

他们也是美国人吗？

　　对，他们都是美国人。

Two students asking each other their nationalities

你是哪国人？

　　我是英国人。你是哪国人？

我是法国人。

　　他也是法国人吗？

对，我们都是法国人。

STEP 2
ABOUT ONE'S HOMETOWN

Looking at the photo of a movie star, two students are talking about his nationality and hometown

他是谁？

　　他是成龙，Jackie Chan。

他是哪国人？

　　他是中国人。

他是中国哪里人？

　　他是中国香港人。

STEP 3
ABOUT WHERE ONE LIVES

Two students learn that they are both from Beijing

小明，你家在哪儿？

　　我家在北京。

我家也在北京！

　　我们是老乡！

你住北京哪儿？

　　我住南边。

我住东边。

lǎoxiāng

someone from the same town/city

Two students exchanging information about where they live

你住哪儿？

　　我住那儿。

住南边？

　　对，住南边。

　　你住哪儿？

我不住南边。我住东边。

Step Up!

1. Prepare a list in Chinese of ten famous people you know today or from history. Information that you will need to collect is shown below. Use *pinyin* if you can't write their nationalities in Chinese. Be sure to include people from at least four different countries (refer to Get Ready).

Name	Gender	Nationality
郎朗	男	中国人
Mariah Carey	女	美国人

2. Work with a classmate to interview each other. Based on the questions provided below, write a short paragraph in Chinese about each other and share it with the class.

❶ 他 / 她叫什么?
   What is his/her name?

❷ 他 / 她是哪国人?
   What is his/her nationality?

❸ 他 / 她家在哪里?
   Where is his/her home?

❹ 他 / 她住哪儿?
   Where does he/she live?

他叫 James Wright. 他是
英国人。他家在 London。
他住 London 西边。

3. Work with a classmate. Practice saying the following dialog with a classmate and perform a simple skit for the class.

你叫什么?

我叫安娜。

❶ 你好!
   你好! 你叫什么?

❷ 我叫小红。
   小红? 你姓什么?

❸ 哦 (ò), 我姓李, 叫李小红。
   李小红, 你是中国人吗?

❹ 对, 我是中国人。你是哪国人? 你叫什么?
   我是美国人。我叫安娜。

❺ 安娜, 你家在哪里?
   我家在纽约。

❻ 你住哪儿?
   我住东边。

❼ 我也住东边。……再见!
   再见!

Fun Time!

Read the following chants about countries with your teacher. See how many countries you can recognize the first time you hear them. Can you tell the similarity between the pronunciations of the names of countries listed in each group?

1

Zhōngguó Hánguó Tàiguó
中国、韩国、泰国
China　South Korea　Thailand

Měiguó Yīngguó Fǎguó
美国、英国、法国
U.S.A.　U.K.　France

2

Hélán　Fēnlán　Bōlán
荷兰、芬兰、波兰
Netherlands　Finland　Poland

Yīnggélán　Sūgélán　Àiěrlán
英格兰、苏格兰、爱尔兰
England　Scotland　Ireland

Xīnxīlán　Wūkèlán　Gélínglán
新西兰、乌克兰、格陵兰
New Zealand　Ukraine　Greenland

3

Jiānà　Jiāpéng　Jiānádà
加纳、加蓬、加拿大
Ghana　Gabon　Canada

Xīnjiāpō　Mèngjiālā　Sàinèijiāěr
新加坡、孟加拉、塞内加尔
Singapore　Bangladesh　Senegal

Tāngjiā　Yámǎijiā　Gēsīdálíjiā
汤加、牙买加、哥斯达黎加
Tonga　Jamaica　Costa Rica

4

Āmàn　Āgēntíng　Āfùhàn
阿曼、阿根廷、阿富汗
Oman　Argentina　Afghanistan

Bāxī　Bānámǎ　Bājīsītǎn
巴西、巴拿马、巴基斯坦
Brazil　Panama　Pakistan

Níbóěr　Nírìlìyà　Níjiālāguā
尼泊尔、尼日利亚、尼加拉瓜
Nepal　Nigeria　Nicaragua

I have learned...

Core Vocabulary

哪 pron.		nǎ	where; which	家[1] n.		jiā	home
国 n.	國	guó	country	在 v.		zài	at
人 n.		rén	person, people	哪儿 pron.	哪兒	nǎr	where
美国人 n.	美國人	Měiguórén	American	这儿 pron.	這兒	zhèr	here
中国人 n.	中國人	Zhōngguórén	Chinese	那儿 pron.	那兒	nàr	there
法国人 n.	法國人	Fǎguórén	French	东 n.	東	dōng	east
英国人 n.	英國人	Yīngguórén	British	西 n.		xī	west
对 adj.	對	duì	yes; right	南 n.		nán	south
不是 phr.		bú shì	no	北 n.		běi	north
也 adv.		yě	also	边 n.	邊	biān	side
都 adv.		dōu	both; all	住 v.		zhù	live
哪里 pron.	哪裏	nǎlǐ	where				

Extended Vocabulary

男 n.	nán	male	女 n.		nǚ	female

Names of Countries

美国	美國	Měiguó	U.S.A	巴西		Bāxī	Brazil
英国	英國	Yīngguó	U.K.	西班牙		Xībānyá	Spain
德国	德國	Déguó	Germany	法国	法國	Fǎguó	France
中国	中國	Zhōngguó	China	南非		Nánfēi	South Africa
日本		Rìběn	Japan	印度		Yìndù	India
墨西哥		Mòxīgē	Mexico	澳大利亚	澳大利亞	Àodàlìyà	Australia

Important Cities in China

北京 Běijīng Beijing		上海 Shànghǎi Shanghai
香港 Xiānggǎng Hong Kong		西安 Xī'ān Xi'an

SENTENCE PATTERNS

你是哪国人？我是美国人。

你是中国人吗？对，我是中国人。/ 不是，我是英国人。

她也是美国人吗？对，我们都是美国人。

你是哪里人？我是北京人。

你家在哪儿？我家在这儿。

你住哪儿？我住东边。

I can do!

Interpretive Communication

❑ I can understand when someone tells me his or her nationality.

❑ I can understand when someone tells me where his or her hometown is.

❑ I can understand when someone tells me where he or she lives.

❑ I can understand yes-no questions.

Interpersonal Communication

❑ I can ask and answer questions about one's nationality.

❑ I can ask and answer questions about where people are from.

❑ I can exchange information about where people live.

Presentational Communication

❑ I can orally describe myself by telling my name, nationality, and where I live.

❑ I can introduce someone and state his or her name, nationality, and where he or she lives.

❑ I can present a short skit about getting to know someone.

❑ I can introduce ten famous people and their nationalities.

Cultural Knowledge

❑ I can explain the Chinese concept of hometown.

❑ I can talk about the things associated with Beijing and Shanghai.

❑ I can identify some celebrities from China and other countries.

❑ I can state the features of a Chinese ID card.

❑ I can identify pictures associated with some Chinese cities.

What time is it?

现在几点?

COMMUNICATIVE GOALS
- Counting and saying numbers
- Reading numbers with decimals
- Stating ordinal numbers
- Talking about different segments of a day
- Asking and telling time

Cultural Knowledge
- Lucky numbers in Chinese culture
- The Chinese abacus
- The Chinese multiplication table
- Sequence of telling time in Chinese
- Chinese hand gestures for numbers

Get ready...

1. Look at these pictures. What numbers do you encounter daily? What numbers do you like and dislike? Why?

2. **Global Connection:** Do you know how to count in other languages? Do you know any lucky and unlucky numbers in other cultures around the world? Do some research on the Internet, and share your findings with the class.

Do you know when the Chinese invented the abacus? What is it used for?

STEPS *at a glance!*

STEP 1

COUNTING AND SAYING NUMBERS

A. From zero through ten
零、一、二……十

B. Numbers in a series
一二零……

C. Double-digit numbers
十一、二十……

D. Numbers from one hundred and above
一百零五……

STEP 2

DIFFERENT TYPES OF NUMBERS

A. Reading numbers with decimals
三点七九

B. Stating ordinal numbers
第一、第二、第三……

STEP 3

DIFFERENT SEGMENTS OF A DAY

A. Segments of a day
上午；中午；下午；晚上

B. Time segments in different days
昨天晚上；明天下午

STEP 4

ASKING AND TELLING TIME

A. Hours
现在几点？现在一点。

B. Minutes and seconds
现在三点零五分十一秒。

C. Quarter and half hour
现在九点一刻；现在两点半

D. Quarter or less
差一刻四点。

71

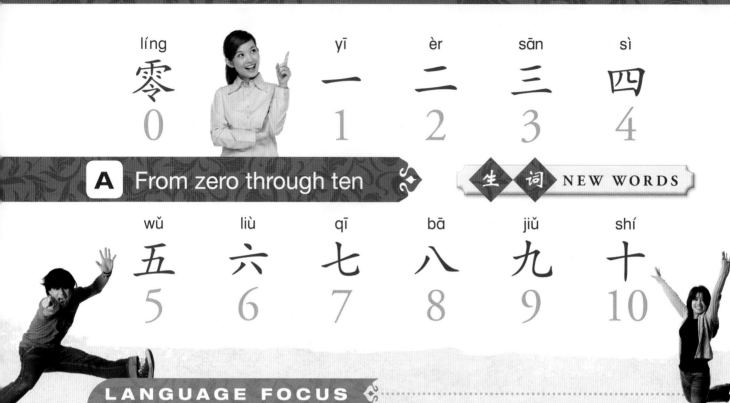

líng
零
0

yī
一
1

èr
二
2

sān
三
3

sì
四
4

A From zero through ten

生 词 NEW WORDS

wǔ
五
5

liù
六
6

qī
七
7

bā
八
8

jiǔ
九
9

shí
十
10

LANGUAGE FOCUS

Learning numbers in Chinese can be easy. Begin by learning to recognize the cardinal characters from 0 through 10 and the rest will follow. You can start to read price tags while shopping, ask for telephone numbers, talk about age, and much more just by learning these simple characters.

There are four basic tones used in pronouncing Chinese characters. The numbers below are grouped according to these four tones. You may find these numbers easier to remember as you try pronouncing them in their respective tones.

1ST TONE

yī	sān	qī	bā
一	三	七	八
1	3	7	8

2ND TONE

líng	shí
零	十
0	10

3RD TONE

wǔ	jiǔ
五	九
5	9

4TH TONE

èr	sì	liù
二	四	六
2	4	6

Try This!

1. Like a rhyme, chant the following characters to practice the four tones:

yī sān qī bā dì yī shēng
一、三、七、八，第一声；
[The first tone]

líng shí shí líng dì èr shēng
零、十、十、零，第二声；
[The second tone]

wǔ jiǔ jiǔ wǔ dì sān shēng
五、九、九、五，第三声；
[The third tone]

èr sì liù èr dì sì shēng
二、四、六、二，第四声。
[The fourth tone]

2. Now from the numbers on the right, see if you can chant them into Chinese for further practice.

1 2 3,   3 2 1,   1 2 3 4 5 6 7.
9 8 7,   6 5 4,   3 2 1.   1 2 3,   4 5 6,   7 8 9.
1 3 5 7 9,   2 4 6 8 10.   1 2 3 4 5 6 7 8 9 10.

3. The illustration depicts a panel from an elevator in a hotel in China. What number is missing? Can you guess why? In your culture, are there numbers that are not used in elevators or seating?

| 8 | 7 | 6 | 5 |
| 3 | 2 | 1 | B1 |

CULTURAL HIGHLIGHTS

Chinese Lucky Numbers: 8, 2, 6, 9

Many Chinese consider **8** a lucky number. In regional dialects, the pronunciation for "eight" and "fortune" sounds similar. For example in Cantonese, **8** is pronounced as "Fatt" as in "Kung Hei **Fatt** Choi", a Chinese New Year's greeting which is also popularly used to wish someone good luck, and good fortune.

Eight is such a powerful number in the Chinese culture. There was once a story of a man in Hangzhou who offered to sell his license plate, A88888, for RMB 1.12 million.

Other Chinese lucky numbers are **2**, **6**, and **9**.

As you might know, many Chinese household decorations come in pairs: two vases, two red candles, two big red lanterns, two stone lions in front of the house, and so on. **Two** symbolizes balance and harmony.

A popular decorative design commonly seen at Chinese weddings is "double happiness," which comprises two stylized characters 喜 (xǐ, happiness).

Six, especially to those who owns businesses, stands for everything will go smoothly without complications.

Nine has a similar pronunciation to the Chinese word 久 (jiǔ, everlasting, longevity). It is also the largest single digit number and is associated with mythical dragons and emperors in the past. Chinese people think that **9** also helps bring lasting relationships and long, blissful lives.

Many Chinese believe that **4** and **7** are unlucky numbers. Find out why.

yāo sān wǔ   èr qī liù bā   sì jiǔ yāo sān
一 三 五　二 七 六 八　四 九 一 三

Example: ...My cell number is 135 2768 4913.

wǔ yāo líng líng bā líng
五 一 零 零 八 零

Example: ...The ZIP code is 510080.

jiǔ bā jiǔ bā
九 八 九 八

Example: ...My license plate number is 9898.

LANGUAGE FOCUS

When saying numbers in a series like your telephone numbers, ID cards, zip codes, or car license plate numbers in Chinese, they are read individually as single digit numbers. The number 1, yī, is often pronounced as yāo by many people in China, especially when saying telephone numbers and/or a series of cardinal numbers. This is to avoid confusion with the number 7, qī, which when said quickly may sound like yī. Try saying yī-qī-qī-yī-èr-bā (177128), and then yāo-qī-qī-yāo-èr-bā quickly to see the difference.

DO YOU KNOW . . . .
你知道吗?

If you are planning a trip to China, knowing some emergency numbers always comes in handy. Below are some of those used in most major Chinese cities. Can you try to say and write them in Chinese? Do you see a pattern in these numbers?

Police: 110 _____

Telephone Information: 114 _____

Ambulance: 120 　一 二 零

Weather: 121 _____

1. Practice by saying in Chinese the following zip codes:

❶ 1 0 0 0 3 7 　　❷ 1 8 6 0 4 4 　　❸ 1 0 0 0 8 1 　　❹ 1 0 7 4 1 2 　　❺ 1 0 8 3 3 9

❻ 五一零零八零　❼ 2 0 0 4 3 3 　　❽ 6 1 1 7 3 1 　　❾ 1 0 7 9 8 3 　　❿ 3 0 7 0 3 3

2. Just like the above exercise, say the following cell numbers and practice pronouncing the number 1 as yāo instead of yī.

❶ 135 7698 3311　❷ 130 3835 6628　❸ 132 0388 8477　❹ 139 9422 6550　❺ 137 8923 5419

❻ 131 2586 9724　❼ 137 2845 9602　❽ 135 5882 7943　❾ 132 5717 8694　❿ 135 6677 8912

3. Can you match the license plate pictures to their corresponding *pinyin*? Fill in the blanks as shown below.

a. èr-yāo-jiǔ-wǔ	f. sān-sān-èr-wǔ-wǔ-wǔ
b. wǔ-líng-líng-jiǔ-bā	g. líng-liù-yāo-jiǔ
c. qī-bā-bā-qī-liù-liù	h. líng-sān-qī-yāo-bā
d. líng-èr-sì-sì-èr	i. sì-qī-sì-líng-sān-liù
e. yāo-bā-èr-jiǔ-qī-líng-bā-bā	j. qī-liù-sì-qī-bā

f

Double-digit numbers

From 11 to 19: take the number 10 and ADD the last digit . . .

11	12	13 →	19
10 + 1 shí yī			
十 + 一 = 十一	十二	十三	十九

For 20, 30, 40 . . . and 90: take the first digit of the number and MULTIPLY it by 10 . . .

20	30	40 →	90
2 x 10 èr shí			
二 x 十 = 二十	三十	四十	九十

For other double-digit numbers above 20. . .

23	39	61	95
èr shí sān			
二十 + 三 = 二十三	三十九	六十一	九十五

CULTURAL HIGHLIGHTS

The Chinese Abacus

The Chinese abacus is based on a system of 10 and is often constructed on a bamboo frame with beads sliding on wooden cylinders. It was used by the Chinese as early as the second century B.C., before the adoption of the written modern numeral system, and is still widely used in China.

The abacus is made up of two portions, the lower and the upper part. To count, you start from the right and work your way to the left. Each bead in the lower part carries a value of 1 while each bead in the upper part carries a value of 5.

Besides Chinese, people from different cultures have developed their own version of the abacus. You may want to do some research on the Internet to learn more.

Try This!

1. Schools in China use a grading system like the one in the left column below. Study it with a classmate. Then each will take a turn to call out five different scores to let the other determine which grades they belong to.

100 (yìbǎi)	A*
90-99	A
80-89	B
70-79	C
60-69	P
59 and below	F

2. Read aloud in Chinese the price on each tag on the following items.

❶ chinese knot — $12

❷ lantern — $18

❸ folding fan — $22

❹ writing brush — $36

❺ boccaro teapot — $48

❻ porcelain plate — $30

❼ reed pipe (a wind instrument) — $86

❽ qipao (traditional Chinese gown) — $99

D Numbers from one hundred and above

yì bǎi
一百
100

yì qiān
一千
1000

yí wàn
一万
10000

LANGUAGE FOCUS

Three-digit numbers are read in this order: first, the value in the hundreds place; second, the value in the tens place; third, the value in the ones place. When there is a zero in a three-digit number, pronounce the zero 零 (líng) if it occupies the tens place. Thus, one hundred and one, 101, is pronounced as yì-bǎi-líng-yī.

Examples:

One hundred and five	105	yì-bǎi-líng-wǔ
One hundred and eleven	111	yì-bǎi-yī-shí-yī
Three hundred and forty six	346	sān-bǎi-sì-shí-liù
Seven hundred and ten	710	qī-bǎi-yī-shí
Nine hundred and ninety nine	999	jiǔ-bǎi-jiǔ-shí-jiǔ

The character for 1,000 is 千 (qiān). A large number like 7,602 is read as qī-qiān-liù-bǎi-líng-èr. And for 10,000 (ten thousand), the character is 万 (wàn). The key to learning how to say large numbers correctly in Chinese is based on how well you understand the different denominations in 万, 千, 百, and 十.

For example:

三千 + 四百 + 八十 + 二
Three thousand, four hundred and eighty two (3,482).

一万 + 五千 + 七百 + 二十 + 三
Fifteen thousand, seven hundred and twenty three (15,723).

When 二 is used before 千 and 万, it is usually changed to the word 两 (liǎng), which also means "two."

For example: ▶ 2,300 两千三百
▶ 25,863 两万五千八百六十三

THE TONE FOR 一

The tone for 一 changes in some instances. When used as cardinal and ordinal numbers, it stays as the first tone, for example, 一 (yī), 二十一 (èr shí yī), 第一 (dìyī).

When followed by a first, second or third tone word, it changes to the fourth tone, such as 一分 (yì fēn), 一年 (yì nián), 一点, (yì diǎn), 一秒 (yì miǎo).

When followed by a fourth tone word, it changes to the second tone, such as 一刻 (yí kè). *(Also see Lesson 1 on tone changes for 不).*

Try This!

1. Say the following numbers in Chinese:

   ❶ 一百零一　　❷ 138　　　　❸ 九百五十七　　❹ 1000　　　❺ 569

   ❻ 3,092　　❼ 五千四百六十三　　❽ 350　　　❾ 109,981　　❿ 7,500

2. Do some research to find out . . .

   ❶ the price of an air ticket from your country to Beijing

   ❷ the total distance covered by the Great Wall

   ❸ the height of Mount Everest

   ❹ the approximate number of students in your school

CONGRATULATIONS
好
You are now an expert in speaking, reading and writing Chinese numbers!

① diǎnr
五点九九

5.99

② 二十七点三五

A Reading numbers with decimals

③ 三十八点九

NEW WORD

点 ¹ *n.* | 點 | diǎnr | dot, point, decimal point

¹ *another meaning appears in Step 4*

LANGUAGE FOCUS

To say a number with decimals in Chinese, use the word 点, which literally means a dot. The numbers after the decimal are read individually.

Examples:

六　点　五　三
This means 6.53.

三　点　七　九
This means 3.79.

Practice by reading the following decimal numbers in Chinese. Then write **⑥** – **⑮** in digits.

① 1.31456

② 18.99

③ 100.256

④ 25.35

⑤ 108.333

⑥ èr-shí-èr-diǎnr-qī

⑦ sān-diǎnr-wǔ

⑧ shí-èr-diǎnr-bā-sān

⑨ líng-diǎnr-qī-sān-wǔ

⑩ yì-bǎi-diǎnr-qī-sì-wǔ

⑪ 一点三五

⑫ 九点七

⑬ 十二点三五八

⑭ 零点零六

⑮ 两百七十四点五

第 dì
一
名 míng
1st

第
二
名
2nd

第
三
名
3rd

NEW WORDS

生词

第 pref.	dì	(used to make an ordinal number)
名 m.w.	míng	(used for position in a competition)
天 n.	tiān	day

◆ LANGUAGE FOCUS

To change a cardinal number to an ordinal number, such as one to the first or two to the second, place 第 before the number, e.g., 第一, 第二, etc.

In the illustration above, 第一名 means the first, 第二名 and 第三名 are the first and second runners-up, respectively.

Try This!

Look at the calendar. Can you change the dates circled into days in the ordinal format?

Look at the example below:

			MAY			
S	M	T	W	T	F	S
1	2	3	4	5	6	7
8	9	10	11	12	13	14
15	16	17	18	19	20	21
22	23	24	25	26	27	28
29	30	31				

dì yī tiān
❶ 第 一 天
Day 1 (of May)

❷ _____
Day 3

❸ _____
Day 6

❹ _____
Day 10

❺ _____
Day 15

❻ _____
Day 19

❼ _____
Day 25

❽ _____
Day 28

Before you get to STEP 4 (Asking and Telling Time), you will need to learn the Chinese terms describing the different segments of a day. The pictures below illustrate morning, noon, afternoon and night.

shàngwǔ	zhōng	xià	wǎnshang
上午	中午	下午	晚上

A Segments of a day

NEW WORDS

上 *prep.*	shàng	up, above	午 *n.*	wǔ	noon
中 *prep.*	zhōng	middle	上午 *n.*	shàngwǔ	morning
下 *prep.*	xià	down, below	中午 *n.*	zhōngwǔ	noon
早上 *n.*	zǎoshang	early morning	下午 *n.*	xiàwǔ	afternoon
			晚上 *n.*	wǎnshang	evening; night

LANGUAGE FOCUS

午 (wǔ) means "noon." In Chinese, 上 means "above," 中 means "middle," and 下 means "below."

When combined with 午 (noon), 上午 literally means "going up to noon time" and refers to the morning; 中午 means "middle of the day," denoting noon; 下午 literally means "coming down from noon" and refers to the afternoon.

To exchange greetings at different times of the day, you can use 好, as previously learned in Lesson 1, together with the words referring to that specific part of the day.

早 上 好！
Good morning!

下 午 好！
Good afternoon!

晚 上 好！
Good evening!

ān
晚 安！
Good night!

Try This!

Look at the pictures. What would be the most appropriate way to greet someone for each situation?

8:00 am
①

4:00 pm
②

8:00 pm
③

6:30 am
④

5:00 pm
⑤

9:00 pm
⑥

B Time segments in different days

zuótiān
昨天晚上
last night

jīn
今天上午
this morning

míng
明天下午
tomorrow afternoon

生词 NEW WORDS

昨天 n.	zuótiān	yesterday
今天 n.	jīntiān	today
明天 n.	míngtiān	tomorrow

LANGUAGE FOCUS

In Chinese, you would say 今天 for today, but if you want to say "this morning," you say 今天上午 (literally means "today morning"). To say last night, you say 昨天晚上, literally meaning "yesterday night" in English. To say "tomorrow afternoon," follow the English pattern and say 明天下午.

Try This!

Arrange the following time segments in the correct sequence:

❶ 今天下午　　❷ 昨天晚上　　❸ 明天中午

❹ 今天中午　　❺ 昨天下午　　❻ 明天早上

ASKING AND TELLING TIME

xiànzài jǐ diǎn
现在几点？
What time is it?

A Hours

现在七点。
It's 7 o'clock sharp.

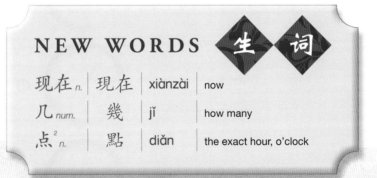

NEW WORDS 生 词

现在 n.	現在	xiànzài	now
几 num.	幾	jǐ	how many
点 2 n.	點	diǎn	the exact hour, o'clock

LANGUAGE FOCUS

When you want to ask what time it is, say "现在几点？" or "几点了(le)？" The answer for that question could be "现在十二点了" or "十二点了。"

Use 点 to refer to the exact hour, e.g., 七点 (*7 o'clock*) and 五点 (*5 o'clock*).

To say 2 o'clock, say 两点 (liǎng diǎn) instead of 二点.

Example: 现 在 几 点 ？ 现 在 两 点 。

Try This!

Match the time shown on the clocks with the time in Chinese characters.

 1 •

• 一点

 2 •

• 五点

 3 •

• 六点

 4 •

• 四点

5 •

• 十点

6 •

• 两点

7 •

• 九点

8 •

• 十一点

9 •

• 八点

10 •

• 七点

11 •

• 十二点

12 •

• 三点

B Minutes and seconds

fēn   miǎo

分   秒

五点三十分、二十一秒。

5 o'clock, 30 minutes and 21 seconds.

生 词

NEW WORDS

| 分 n. | fēn | minute |
| 秒 n. | miǎo | second |

LANGUAGE FOCUS

The sequence for telling time in Chinese follows the Chinese cultural concept of viewing things from big to small. In Chinese, we say the day first, followed by the part of the day (as AM or PM), then the exact hour, minutes or seconds.

Examples:

▸ 3:25 PM today
今天下午三点二十五 (分)

▸ 11:05 AM yesterday
昨天上午十一点零五 (分)

When stating minutes from 1 to 9, use 零 to represent "0." It is optional to use 分 in stating minutes.

Examples:

❶ 现在几点?
现在三点零五 (分)。
It is 3:05.

❷ 现在几点?
现在两点十五 (分)。
It is 2:15.

Try This!

Look at the time on the digital clock and tell your partner what time is displayed. Take turns telling each other the time you see on the clock.

① 03:30:25

② 11:23:30

③ 10:43:45

④ 04:15:06

⑤ 05:58:55

⑥ 01:27:35

⑦ 12:27:20

⑧ 02:34:59

⑨ 07:45:18

⑩ 10:05:19

DO **YOU** KNOW . . .
你知道吗?

In China, radio announcements and signs posted at public places like airports, train stations, and bus terminals often use a 24-hour clock. Time is displayed in the format "**hours : minutes : seconds**." For example: 13:31:42 means 1:31:42 PM. Midnight is called 零点, and 8:00 PM would be 二十点.

Even though China covers a vast geographic area, it maintains one time zone, called Chinese Standard Time or Beijing Time. It is the Greenwich Mean Time, plus 8 hours (GMT+8).

Quarter and half hour

六点三刻 ^{kè}

六点三刻
6:45 or a quarter to 7:00

六点一刻 ^{kè}
6:15 or a quarter past 6:00

六点半 ^{bàn}
Half past 6:00 or 6:30

NEW WORDS 生 词

| 刻 n. | kè | quarter of an hour |
| 半 n. | bàn | half; half of an hour |

LANGUAGE FOCUS

Instead of saying 15 minutes (十五分) after the hour, you can use the word 刻 to refer to the time in the quarter segment of an hour. As in English, you may say 一刻 (one quarter) and 三刻 (three quarters), but you cannot say "two quarters of an hour." Use 半 to represent the half hour. Here are examples of the use of 刻 and 半:

9:15:	九点十五分	or	九点一刻
7:45:	七点四十五分	or	七点三刻
2:30:	两点三十分	or	两点半
10:30:	十点三十分	or	十点半

Here are some sample dialogs on different ways of asking questions about time:

❶ 几 点 了 ?   三 点 一 刻 了 。

What time is it?   It is 3:15 now.

❷ 现 在 几 点 ?   现 在 两 点 三 刻 。

                  It is 2:45 now.

❸ 现 在 几 点 ?   现 在 十 一 点 半 。

                  It is 11:30 now.

Below is David's daily schedule. Read out the time for each activity in Chinese.

My daily routine

Getting Up	6:45 am
Eating Breakfast	7:15 am
Going to School	7:30 am
Class Begins	8:00 am
Having Lunch	11:45 am
Going Home	4:30 pm
Doing Homework	5:15 pm
Having Dinner	6:45 pm
Leisure Activities	7:30 pm
Going to Bed	9:15 pm

D Quarter or less

chà

差五分一点

Five minutes to one

NEW WORD

差 v. | chà | be short of, lack of

LANGUAGE FOCUS

To say "It is five minutes to ten," you may say "差五分十点." The word 差 means "short of," and the number after 差 should be fewer than 15 minutes. For example: 差一刻四点 means "a quarter to four." The actual time referred to here is 三点四十五分 (3:45).

3:45	差 一 刻 四 点
7:50	差 十 分 八 点

Look at these examples:

❶ 几 点 了?　　三 点 了。
It is 3:00 o'clock.

❷ 几 点 了?　　差 十 分 五 点 了。
It is 10 minutes to 5:00.

1. Use 差 to say the following times:

❶ 10:55 ❷ 2:45 ❸ 8:50 ❹ 9:53 ❺ 6:58 ❻ 11:49

2. Look at the example shown below. Convert the following times from a 24-hour clock to a 12-hour clock. Read both times aloud in Chinese.

24-hour Clock	< 2:00 PM >	12-hour Clock
shí sì diǎn 十 四 点		xiàwǔ liǎng diǎn 下 午 两 点

❶ 13:10 ❷ 13:40 ❸ 14:20 ❹ 15:30 ❺ 16:45 ❻ 17:15
❼ 18:35 ❽ 19:00 ❾ 20:20 ❿ 21:00 ⓫ 22:19 ⓬ 23:48

3. Look at the "score board" below. Imagine you are a score reader. Read out loud the names of the athletes, the countries they belong to and the time of their scores using 秒.

SUPER GRAND PRIX, *Lausanne (2006)*
110m Hurdles

❶	Liu Xiang	China	12.88 s
❷	Arnold	USA	12.90 s
❸	Trammell	USA	13.02 s
❹	Robies	Cuba	13.04 s
❺	Merritt	USA	13.12 s
❻	Olijar	Latvia	13.19 s
❼	Doucoure	France	13.36 s

DIALOG *in Context*

STEP 1
COUNTING AND SAYING NUMBERS

Read this Chinese rhyme

一二三四五六七，
我的朋友在哪里？
在这里，在这里，
我的朋友在这里。

de
a structural particle that indicates possession or close association

Read the following numbers in Chinese

A social security number...

六一二　六五　四三二零
6 1 2　6 5　4 3 2 0

A car license plate number...

六三二八九
6 3 2 8 9

A telephone number...

六五零　八五七　零三二九
6 5 0　8 5 7　0 3 2 9

STEP 2
DIFFERENT TYPES OF NUMBERS

Read the following decimal numbers in Chinese

五十七点八　57.8
三十六点二　36.2
二十九点四　29.4

After a track and field event, two friends are talking about the scores

John 是第几名？
　　第三名。
很好！马丁是第几名？
　　第一名！

STEP 3
DIFFERENT SEGMENTS OF A DAY

Read out Lily's leisure schedule in Chinese

To the movies...
　　昨天晚上

Ballet class...
　　今天上午

Playing tennis...
　　明天下午

STEP 4
ASKING AND TELLING TIME

Read out David's school day schedule in Chinese

Meeting the coach...
　　七点一刻 (七点十五分)

Class starts...
　　七点三刻 (七点四十五分)

Lunch break...
　　十二点半

Biology quiz...
　　两点

Class ends...
　　四点二十分

Step Up!

1. Here is a Chinese math challenge for you! Read the value of "π" out loud. Try to say the numbers as fast as you can:

> 3.14159 26535 89793 23846 26433 83279 50288 41971 69399 37510
> 58209 74944 59230 78164 06286 20899 86280 34825 34211 70679

2. In China, students recite the following multiplication tables. With a partner, read the tables by alternating each number or each column. The word 得 (dé) means *gets* or *equals*.

1 x 1 = 1

一一得一	二二得四	三三得九	四四十六	五五二十五
一二得二	二三得六	三四十二	四五二十	五六三十
一三得三	二四得八	三五十五	四六二十四	五七三十五
一四得四	二五一十	三六十八	四七二十八	五八四十
一五得五	二六十二	三七二十一	四八三十二	五九四十五
一六得六	二七十四	三八二十四	四九三十六	
一七得七	二八十六	三九二十七		
一八得八	二九十八			
一九得九				

六六三十六	七七四十九	八八六十四	九九八十一
六七四十二	七八五十六	八九七十二	
六八四十八	七九六十三		
六九五十四			

9 x 9 = 81

3. Create a time schedule of your average day with at least 10 things that you do. On the schedule, write out the time in numbers and in Chinese, then write the activities you do in English. Be sure to include times for these six activities: getting up, eating breakfast, going to school, coming home from school, doing homework, and going to bed. You may choose the other four and may have more activities for your day.

What time?	几点?	My daily routine
6:00 AM	早上六点	Getting up

Fun Time!

1. Choose a partner and practice counting numbers with hand signals shown below. Read out loud in Chinese while counting.

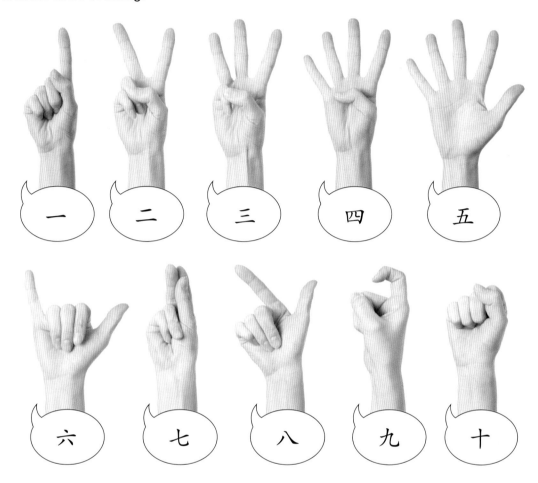

2. Practice the following rhyme.

一 二 三 ， 三 二 一 ， 一 二 三 四 五 六 七 。

一 二 三 ， 三 二 一 ， 七 六 五 四 三 二 一 。

shǔ   cóng   dào

你 数 八 ， 我 数 九 。 从 一 数 到 十 。

You count to 8. I count to 9. Let's count from 1 through 10.

一 二 三 四 五 ， 六 七 八 九 十 。

I have learned...

NEW WORDS

Core Vocabulary

零 *num.*	líng	zero		万 *num.*	萬	wàn	ten thousand
一 *num.*	yī	one		点¹ *n.*	點	diǎn	dot, point, decimal point
二 *num.*	èr	two		第 *pref.*		dì	*(used to make an ordinal number)*
三 *num.*	sān	three		名 *m.w.*		míng	*(used for position in a competition)*
四 *num.*	sì	four		天 *n.*		tiān	day
五 *num.*	wǔ	five		现在 *n.*	現在	xiànzài	now
六 *num.*	liù	six		几 *num.*	幾	jǐ	how many
七 *num.*	qī	seven		点² *n.*	點	diǎnr	the exact hour, o'clock
八 *num.*	bā	eight		分 *n.*		fēn	minute of an hour
九 *num.*	jiǔ	nine		秒 *n.*		miǎo	second of a minute
十 *num.*	shí	ten		刻 *n.*		kè	quarter of an hour
百 *num.*	bǎi	hundred		半 *n.*		bàn	half; half of an hour
千 *num.*	qiān	thousand		差 *v.*		chà	be short of, lack of

Extended Vocabulary

午 *n.*	wǔ	noon		早上 *n.*	zǎoshang	morning
上 *prep.*	shàng	up; above		晚上 *n.*	wǎnshang	evening
中 *prep.*	zhōng	middle		今天 *n.*	jīntiān	today
下 *prep.*	xià	down; below		昨天 *n.*	zuótiān	yesterday
上午 *n.*	shàngwǔ	morning		明天 *n.*	míngtiān	tomorrow
中午 *n.*	zhōngwǔ	noon		晚安 *phr.*	wǎn'ān	good night
下午 *n.*	xiàwǔ	afternoon				

SENTENCE PATTERNS

现在几点？	现在六点二十五分。	现在八点半。
现在七点。	现在三点三刻。	现在差一刻四点。

I can do!

Interpretive **Communication**

❏ I can read and recognize numbers 1 – 1000.

❏ I can understand some ordinal numbers.

❏ I can understand when someone says numbers to me from 1 – 1000.

❏ I can understand when someone presents numbers with hand signals.

❏ I can understand when someone tells me the time.

❏ I can read zip codes and phone numbers.

Interpersonal **Communication**

❏ I can ask and tell time on a 12-hour and 24-hour clock.

❏ I can ask and answer questions about segments of time in a day.

❏ I can greet people according to the time of day.

Presentational **Communication**

❏ I can count to 10 in Chinese.

❏ I can say some ordinal numbers.

❏ I can show numbers using hand gestures.

❏ I can state decimal numbers.

❏ I can tell time on different clocks.

Cultural Knowledge

❏ I can state what numbers are lucky for Chinese people.

❏ I can roughly understand how an abacus works.

❏ I can read the Chinese multiplication table.

❏ I can tell time in Chinese using the correct sequence.

❏ I can talk about the grading system in China.

❏ I can compare Chinese and American hand gestures for numbers.

What's todays date?

今天几号？

COMMUNICATIVE GOALS

- Talking about the year, month, week and day
- Stating a specific period of time
- Asking someone's age and birthday
- Using tag questions
- Expressing well wishes

Cultural Knowledge

- The Chinese lunar calendar
- The evolution of pictographic characters 月 and 日
- The proper way to ask a Chinese person's age
- Common Chinese expressions of good wishes
- Dates of major Chinese festivals
- The 24 solar terms

Get ready...

Global Connection: The WORLD'S IMPORTANT DAYS are marked on the calendar to observe issues that are of concern around the world. The international community and the United Nations take these days very seriously and use them to commemorate historical events, promote activities, and mobilize people to action.

Below is a table depicting twelve such important days. Find out on the Internet what dates they take place on, and what they mean. Choose at least two days and discuss with a classmate why you think they are important.

CALENDAR OF *World's* IMPORTANT DAYS

JANUARY

World Peace Day

FEBRUARY

Valentine's Day

MARCH

International Women's Day

APRIL

Earth Day

MAY

Labor Day

JUNE

World Environment Day

JULY

World Nature Conservation Day

AUGUST

International Youth Day

SEPTEMBER

World Tourism Day

OCTOBER

United Nations Day

NOVEMBER

World Hello Day

DECEMBER

World Aids Day

STEP 1

YEAR, MONTH, WEEK AND DAY

A. About the year
今年是2015年。

B. About the month
一月、二月、三月······

C. About days in a month
今天几号？今天二月十五号。

D. About days in a week
今天星期几？今天星期五。

E. Sequencing months and weeks
上个月；下个星期

STEP 2

COUNTING YEARS, MONTHS, WEEKS AND DAYS

A. Counting years and days
三年；七天

B. Counting months and weeks
两个月；四个星期

STEP 3

AGE AND BIRTHDAY

A. Asking one's age
你多大？ / 你几岁？

B. Asking one's birthday
你的生日是几月几号？

C. Asking tag questions
你呢？ / 你的呢？

D. Expressing well wishes
祝你生日快乐！

STEP 1
YEAR, MONTH, WEEK AND DAY

 生 词 NEW WORDS

qiánnián	qùnián	jīnnián	míngnián	hòunián
前年	去年	今年	明年	后年
year before last	last year	this year	next year	year after next

A About the year

The year 年 is an important concept in dates. To refer to the current year, or the year before or after the current year, we add a modifier before 年:

Examples:

去年　今年　明年

To refer to a specific year, we state the series of numbers representing the year before 年:

Examples:

2014 年 2015 年 2016 年

LANGUAGE FOCUS

Note that in Chinese, the four-digit number for a year is read digit-by-digit.

Examples:

1995 年　一九九五年
　　　　　yī-jiǔ-jiǔ-wǔ-nián

2015 年　二〇一五年
　　　　　èr-líng-yī-wǔ-nián

 CULTURAL HIGHLIGHTS

The Chinese Lunar Calendar

The Chinese lunar calendar is based on the cycles of the moon. Chinese define a month with the waxing and waning of the moon which usually takes 29 or 30 days. There are 12 months in a lunar year, making up to 354 or 355 days in total.

The Chinese lunar calendar plays an important role in the lives of Chinese people. Traditional Chinese festivals follow the lunar calendar. The Chinese New Year falls on the first day of the first lunar month, the Dragon Boat Festival the fifth day of the fifth lunar month, and the Mid-Autumn Festival the fifteenth day of the eighth lunar month.

Even in present time, the lunar calendar is still being used by many Chinese as a way of remembering important dates and festivals, as well as determining auspicious dates for celebrations.

100

1. Read aloud the following in Chinese. Follow the speech pattern shown below:

yī qī sān liù nián
1736年：一七三六年

1 2008 年　　**2** 2012 年　　**3** 2009 年　　**4** 1999 年
5 2010 年　　**6** 1945 年　　**7** 2011 年　　**8** 2000 年

2. Starting from the current year, complete the following in Chinese.

前年
1

去年
2

今年
3

明年
4

后年
5

3. Below is a picture of a typical Chinese lunar calendar and a Gregorian calendar. Spend some time studying the various features of each calendar. Next, see if you can pick out at least two similarities and differences between them. Share your findings with the class.

Year of the Goat 羊年　　December 2015　二〇一五年十二月

MON 星期一	TUE 星期二	WED 星期三	THU 星期四	FRI 星期五	SAT 星期六	SUN 星期日
1 二十	**2** 廿一	**3** 廿二	**4** 廿三	**5** 廿四	**6** 廿五	
7 大雪	**8** 廿七	**9** 廿八	**10** 廿九	**11** 初一	**12** 初二	**13** 初三

DECEMBER 2015

SUN	MON	TUE	WED	THU	FRI	SAT
		1	2	3	4	5
6	7	8	9	10	11	12

B About the month

生 词 NEW WORDS

yuè 一 月 January	二 月 February	三 月 March
四 月 April	五 月 May	六 月 June
七 月 July	八 月 August	九 月 September
十 月 October	十 一 月 November	十 二 月 December

LANGUAGE FOCUS

To name the months in Chinese is easy. Just simply say the number between one to twelve with the word 月 (yuè), which means a month. So, 一月 (yīyuè) is January, 二月 (èryuè) is February and so on.

102

STEP UP WITH CHINESE • 成长

You will need a calendar, preferably one that incorporates lunar dates, for the following exercises.

1. Work with a classmate and take turns. Point to a month on the calendar and let your classmate say what month it is.

2. Work with a classmate. Find out the answers and practice by saying them in Chinese:

   ❶ The current month
   ❷ The month of your birthday
   ❸ The month of your classmate's birthday
   ❹ The month of your mid-term examination
   ❺ The month you like most
   ❻ The month you will go on winter break

3. Using your calendar, find out the month on which each of the following festivals is celebrated. Practice with a classmate by saying the month aloud.

   ❶ Valentine's Day ⟶ 二月
   ❷ New Year's Day
   ❸ Labor Day
   ❹ Mother's Day
   ❺ Dragon Boat Festival
   ❻ Father's Day
   ❼ Thanksgiving Day
   ❽ Mid-Autumn Festival
   ❾ National Day of your country

CULTURAL HIGHLIGHTS

The Month and the Moon

The character 月 stands for both "moon" and "month." In ancient times, Chinese people used the moon to tell time. The waxing and waning of the moon represents a month.

The illustration below shows the evolution of the character for moon. It began as a pictograph of the crescent moon and changed its form through the various scripts in different eras.

| oracle bone script c. 1600 - 1046 B.C. | inscription on bronze objects c. 1400 - 221 B.C. | seal script c. 221 B.C. - 25 A.D. | regular script 25 A.D. - present |

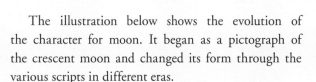

前天	zuó 昨天	今天	明天	后天
day before yesterday	yesterday	today	tomorrow	day after tomorrow
SATURDAY	**SUNDAY**	**MONDAY**	**TUESDAY**	**WEDNESDAY**

jǐ hào
今天几号?
What is today's date?

今天(三月)三号。
It is the third (of March) today.

NEW WORDS

号 n.	號	hào	number; date (spoken)
日 n.		rì	day; date (written)

LANGUAGE FOCUS

When to use 号 or 日? We may use either 号 or 日 to express the day in dates. 号 is more often used in spoken language whereas 日 is often used in formal, written documents, and often in conjunction with the month, e.g. 六月一日.

When asking and answering questions about time and dates, it is not necessary to put 是 in the sentence.

Examples:

	Questions	Answers
❶	今天几号?	今天三号。
❷	明天几号?	明天八号。

The vast majority of the world's countries uses the "Day-Month-Year" date format. The "Month-Day-Year" format is used primarily in the United States. The Chinese date format has the largest data item written before the smaller data item, i.e. year before month before day.

Examples:　❶ 一九九九年三月五日 (March 5th, 2010)
　　　　　　❷ 二〇一二年五月一号 (May 1st, 2012)
　　　　　　❸ 二〇一五年十月十七号 (October 17th, 2015)

1. From the list below, circle the dates that you think are more likely used in Chinese written documents:

❶ 5月1号　❷ 5月12日　❸ 6月8日　❹ 5月12号　❺ 8月3号　❻ 7月5号　❼ 2月1日

❽ 7月5日　❾ 8月3日　❿ 5月1号　⓫ 5月1日　⓬ (10月1日)　⓭ 10月1号　⓮ 3月3号

2. From the list below, circle the dates that are in the format mostly used in China. Next, read the dates you circled aloud in Chinese. There is an erroneous date in the list. Can you spot it?

❶ 2/6/2011　❷ 6/1/2000　❸ 1980.6.23　❹ 1983.12.1　❺ 2010.11.8　❻ 15/1/1999

❼ (2006.7.1)　❽ 2013.2.13　❾ 25/3/2000　❿ 2001.25.3　⓫ 2001.3.25　⓬ 2011.5.28

二〇〇六年七月一号

3. Bring a calendar. Your teacher will point to a date on the calendar and ask questions based on the speech pattern shown here:

> Teacher: 今天几号？／明天几号？／昨天几号？／
> 前天几号？／后天几号？

Next, provide answers to the questions based on the speech pattern shown here:

> Student: 今天……号。／明天……号。／昨天……号。／
> 前天……号。／后天……号。

4. Study the example and fill in the missing information in the chart below.

前天	昨天	今天	明天	后天
三月一日	三月二日	三月三日	三月四日	三月五日 ✓
			四月十二日	
				五月十日
		八月一日		
	十一月二十日			

5. Look at the sample of a train ticket below. Notice which word (号 or 日) is used in the date. Answer the questions on the right.

A012345   上海 🔴

上海   T104次   北京
Shanghai   ➤   Beijing
2012 年 12 月 25 日   20:36开   09 车 013 号下铺
¥283.00 元   新空调硬座快速卧
限乘当日当次车
在 3 日内到有效

1234567 W011274 2456788900486422457755444385345678654479089776

❶ What is the train departure date?

❷ What is the train departure time?

❸ How much does the ticket cost?

❹ What is the car (车 chē) and seat number printed on the ticket?

❺ Which two cities does this train shuttle between?

 CULTURAL HIGHLIGHTS

日 is a pictogram that depicts the sun. It is also an ideogram in which the meaning of "a day" is expressed iconically, as the rising and setting of the sun marks one day. Therefore, besides the moon, Chinese also used the sun to tell the passage of time.

The Sun and the Day

The illustration shows how the character 日 has evolved over the years. The earliest form took the image of the sun and evolved through the various ancient scripts to its present form.

oracle bone script c. 1600 - 1046 B.C.	inscription on bronze objects c. 1400 - 221 B.C.	seal script c. 221 B.C. - 25 A.D.	regular script 25 A.D. - present
⊝ →	⊝ →	𐊗 →	日

生 词 NEW WORDS

xīngqī

星期一	星期二	星期三	星期四	星期五	星期六	星期日
MONDAY	TUESDAY	WEDNESDAY	THURSDAY	FRIDAY	SATURDAY	SUNDAY

lunch Specials this week!

今天星期几？
What day is today?

今天星期五。
It's Friday!

◆ LANGUAGE FOCUS

The Chinese word for week is 星期. The days of the week from Monday through Saturday is named using the numbers one to six (i.e. 星期一 is Monday), with the exception of Sunday which is named as 星期天 or 星期日. Another word for week is 周 (zhōu). We can use 星期 and 周 interchangeably, e.g. 周一 is the same as 星期一.

To ask which day of the week it is, put the question word 几 in place of the day to form the question.

Example: 今天星期几？
今天星期三。

With a calendar, work with a classmate and take turns to ask and answer the following questions. Say the dialogs aloud to practice the dates and days of the week.

❶ 今天几月几号，星期几？
今天_____月_____号，星期_____。

❷ 前天几月几号？星期几？
前天_____月_____号，星期_____。

❸ 昨天几月几号？星期几？
昨天_____月_____号，星期_____。

❹ 明天几月几号？星期几？
明天_____月_____号，星期_____。

❺ 后天几月几号？星期几？
后天_____月_____号，星期_____。

gè

上 个 月
last month
上個月

zhè / zhèi

这 个 月
current month
這個月

下 个 月
next month
下個月

生 词 NEW WORDS

上 个 星 期
last week
上個星期

Last week I took the
final examination.

这 个 星 期
current week
這個星期

This week our grades
came back. I did well!

下 个 星 期
next week
下個星期

Next week we will go on
a summer vacation. :)

LANGUAGE FOCUS

In Chinese, measure words are always used when counting or specifying nouns.

Month (月) and week (星期) are measured by the measure word 个. To refer to the current, previous or next month/year, you would use the Chinese word 这 (this), 上 (previous) and 下 (next) with the measure word 个. The same is applicable to days of the week.

Examples: 这个月 (this month), 这个星期 (this week)

上个月 (last month), 上个星期五 (last Friday)

下个星期 (next week), 下个星期天 (next Sunday)

More examples: ❶ 这个月是几月？这个月是四月。
What month is it? It is April.

❷ 上个月是几月？上个月是三月。
What was last month? It was March.

❸ 下个月是几月？下个月是五月。
What is next month? It is May.

❹ 这个星期五是几号？这个星期五是八号。
What is the date this Friday? It will be the eighth.

❺ 上个星期天是几号？上个星期天是三号。
What was the date last Sunday? It was the third.

❻ 下个星期六是几号？下个星期六是九号。
What is the date next Saturday? It will be the ninth.

Try This!

1. Study the example and fill in the missing information in the chart below.

上个月	这个月	下个月
二月	三月	四月 ✓
五月		
		一月
	二月	
	十一月	

2. With the help of a calendar, answer the following questions. Next, practice by reading aloud the questions and answers.

❶ 这个星期二是几号？ 这个星期二是十一号。

❷ 上个月是几月？

❸ 下个星期三是几号？

❹ 下个月是几月？

❺ 上周三是几号？

❻ 这个月是几月？

❼ 上个星期三是几号？

❽ 下个星期五是几号？

When you say or count the number of years, add the numeral characters before 年.

十二年

一百年

五千年
5000 years

A Counting years and days

Just like 年, when you say or count the number of days, add the numeral characters before 天.

七天

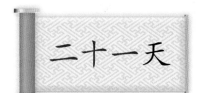
二十一天

三百六十五天
365 days

LANGUAGE FOCUS

年 and 天 are referred to as a unit or a period of time. There is no need to use a measure word when you are stating the number of years or days.

Now, can you guess how to say half a day and half a year? Use the word 半 (bàn) that you have learned previously.

B Counting months and weeks

Naming months!
As in January, February, March, April and so on . . .

Counting months!
As in one, five, twelve months and so on . . .

一月

一个月

五月

五个月

十二月

十二个月

LANGUAGE FOCUS

Unlike 年 and 天 where no measure word is needed, when you count the number of months, you need to use the measure word 个 right after the number. Look at the illustration above. It explains the difference between naming a month and counting months. Similarly, when you are counting weeks, use the same measure word 个 right after the number.

两个星期

十个星期

十二个星期

Try This!

1. Work with a classmate to answer the following questions in Chinese.

   ❶ How many weeks are there in the school year?

   ❷ How many months are there in summer vacation?

   ❸ How many months are there in this remaining school year?

   ❹ How many years have you been studying at your present school?

   ❺ How many days are there in a lunar month?

   ❻ How many days are there in a lunar year?

   ❼ How many weeks of school vacation do you have in a year?

   ❽ How many public holidays does your country have?

2. Study the calendar below and answer the following questions in Chinese.

SUN	MON	TUE	WED	THU	FRI	SAT
1	2	3	4	5	6	7
8	9	10	11	12	13	14
15	today	17	18	19	20	21
22	23	24	25	26	27	28
29	30	31				

   ❶ How many days are there in the month?

   ❷ How many weeks are there in the month?

   ❸ How many days are there in the remaining week?

   ❹ How many weeks have passed for this month?

   ❺ What is today's date on the calendar?

AGE AND BIRTHDAY

In Chinese culture, there are different ways to ask someone his/her age. Here are some examples:

你几岁？

我八岁。
I am eight.

Use this when asking the age of someone young.

A Asking one's age

NEW WORDS

岁 n.	歲	suì	year of age
多大 phr.	多大	duō dà	how old
年纪 n.	年紀	niánjì	age

你多大？

我二十一岁。
I am twenty-one.

Use this when asking the age of an adult or peer.

您多大年纪？

我七十岁。
I am seventy.

Use this when asking the age of an elderly person.

Try This!

1. Look at the example. Answer the following questions based on the information provided. Read out loud both questions and answers when you have completed these exercises.

❶ 她几岁？   她四岁。
_____ 。（4岁）

❷ 你弟弟几岁？
_____ 。（9岁）

❸ 安琪多大？
_____ 。（16岁）

❹ 马克多大？
_____ 。（15岁）

❺ 他爸爸多大？
_____ 。（42岁）

 nǎinai
❻ 你奶奶多大年纪？ _____ 。（79岁）
 grandmother

2. Look at the pictures and guess how old these people are. Work with a classmate to ask and answer questions about the age of these people using the appropriate speech pattern.

她几岁？
她三岁。

![dragon] **CULTURAL HIGHLIGHTS**

The Proper Way to Ask a Chinese Person's Age

Although not a common practice in the West, in Chinese culture, it is common and acceptable to ask an elderly person his/her age. However, it must be done properly. The polite way to ask is:

您多大年纪(了)？

Many Chinese are proud of reaching old age, and Chinese culture reveres older members of the community and older relatives. Asking an older person's age is seen as a sign of concern and respect.

de shēngrì
你 的 生 日 是 几 月 几 号 ？

When is your birthday?

我 的 生 日 是 七 月 二 十 号 。

My birthday is on the 20th of July.

生 词

NEW WORDS

的 *part.*	de	*(used after an attributive)*
生日 *n.*	shēngrì	birthday

LANGUAGE FOCUS

The particle 的 is most commonly used as a possessive modifier. It can be used between two nouns to indicate a relationship of possessor and posession.

Examples: 我的生日
爸爸的年纪
安琪的家

But when personal pronouns (我, 你, 他) are used to qualify kinship terms, 的 is often omitted.

Examples: 我爸爸……
他妈妈……

Now, you can put together what you have learned so far to express someone's birthday.

Examples:

我爸爸的生日是九月十一号。
他妈妈的生日是十二月三十号。

1. Make up complete sentences to tell the birthdays of the people listed. The first number in the brackets represents the month and the second number the date.

❶ 安琪（九 / 二十四）　　安琪的生日是九月二十四日　　　。

❷ 马克（十一 / 九）　　　_____。

❸ 我爸爸（八 / 八）　　　_____。

❹ 我们的老师（十一 / 二十六）_____。

❺ 我的朋友（六 / 十二）　　_____。

❻ 她妈妈（三 / 三十）　　　_____。

❼ 我（五 / 二十二）　　　　_____。

❽ 安琪的爸爸（七 / 十五）　_____。

2. Go around the classroom to complete this survey in Chinese. You will need to ask at least five classmates what their names are and when their birthdays are, and then write down the answers. Follow the two question samples shown below:

Question 1: 你叫什么名字？

Question 2: 你的生日是几月几号？

Name	Birthday
李明	李明的生日是三月二十五日。

C Asking tag questions

我的生日是九月二十四号。
My birthday is on September 24th.

ne
你的呢？
What about yours?

NEW WORD

呢 *part.* | ne | (*used to form questions*)

LANGUAGE FOCUS

I enjoy learning Chinese and speaking in Mandarin. How about you?

"你呢？" or "你的呢？" is a tag question similar to "*How about you?*" in the above example. There are two ways to form a tag question with 呢.

First, when the subject in the preceding sentence is a person, 呢 is used with a pronoun or proper noun to form a tag question.

Examples: ❶ 他是马克。她呢？
He is Mark. Who is she?

❷ 我是中国人。芳芳呢？
I am Chinese. What about Fangfang?

Second, when the subject in the preceding sentence is related to a person, 呢 is used with a possessive pronoun to form a tag question.

Examples: ❸ 我的生日是九月四号。你的呢？
My birthday is on September 4th. What about yours?

Try This!

1. Add a tag question to each of the following sentences.

❶ 我是美国人。   你呢？ 。 ❺ 她是安琪。 _____ 。

❷ 他的生日是八月八号。 _____ 。 ❻ 我叫王大卫。 _____ 。

❸ 我很忙。 _____ 。 ❼ 她的生日是三月九号。 _____ 。

❹ 他姓张。 _____ 。

zhù　　　　kuàilè
祝你生日快乐!
(Wishing you a) Happy Birthday!

jiérì
祝你节日快乐!
(Wishing you a) Happy Holiday!

生词

NEW WORDS

祝 v.	zhù	wish
快乐 adj.	快樂 kuàilè	happy; joyful
节日 n.	節日 jiérì	festival; holiday

◆ LANGUAGE FOCUS

Birthdays and festive holidays are often occasions when we wish others happiness and success. Chinese would start off by saying such greetings with 祝你…… / 我祝你…… (Wishing you… / I wish you…).

DO **YOU** KNOW...
你知道吗?

Other Chinese expressions for best wishes include:

xīnnián
❶ 祝你新年快乐!
Happy New Year!

hǎoyùn
❷ 祝你好运!
Good luck!

shēntǐ jiànkāng
❸ 祝你身体健康!
I wish you the best of health!

zhōumò yúkuài
❹ 祝你周末愉快!
Have a great weekend!

yílù píngān
❺ 祝你一路平安!
Have a safe trip!

chénggōng
❻ 祝你成功!
I wish you success!

Challenge Yourself: What would you say to the person under the given scenario described in each picture?

祝你好运!

❶ Angie is taking a test today.

❷ It is Xiaoli's mother's birthday.

❸ Mike is going to see the terra cotta statues in Xi'an.

❹ It is Friday afternoon and Tony is leaving school.

❺ It is Mary's birthday and you run into her.

❻ You are toasting to the future.

❼ It is January 1st.

❽ Mike's father is going to the hospital for a checkup.

❾ David is traveling to another city to visit his grandmother.

STEP 1
YEAR, MONTH, WEEK AND DAY

Two friends talking about the coming Chinese New Year

现在是几月？
　　一月。

今天几号？
　　一月十六号。

今天星期几？
　　星期一。

下个星期是春节吗？
　　对！是二〇一二年
的春节。

Chūn Jié
Spring Festival/
Chinese New Year

STEP 2
COUNTING YEARS, MONTHS, WEEKS AND DAYS

Students talking about the year, month, week and day

一年有几个月？
　　有十二个月。

一年有多少天？
　　有三百六十五天。

一个月有多少天？
　　有三十天。

一个月有几个星期？
　　四个星期。

一个星期有几天？
　　有七天。

yǒu
have, there is/are

duōshǎo
how many/much

STEP 3
AGE AND BIRTHDAY

Students talking about age and birthday

今天星期几？
　　今天星期五。
明天是我奶奶的生日。星期六，
十月十六号。
　　是吗？祝她生日快乐！
谢谢！
　　她多大年纪？
八十岁了。你的生日是几月几号？
　　我的生日是十一月二十五
号。下个月！

哦！你多大？
　　我二十一岁。
我今年也二十一岁！

ò
oh

Step Up!

1. **Research and discover:** Why do people around the world celebrate festivals and commemorate certain days, events or seasons? Here is an opportunity to learn more about the Chinese people and their culture. Below are some Chinese festivals and events commemorated annually. Go to the library or Internet to search for information. Organize your findings into a chart like this:

Picture	Name	Date
	春节	

① Guóqìng Jié
国庆节

② Chūn Jié
春节

③ Duānwǔ Jié
端午节

④ Zhōngqiū Jié
中秋节

⑤ Qīngmíng Jié
清明节

⑥ Jiàoshī Jié
教师节

2. Create greeting cards for senior citizens. Include a bilingual greeting message in Chinese and English. Visit a senior citizen center near you with the cards you have created. Spread the joy of what you have learned with them. Below are some ideas for your cards.

Here you can practice greeting them by saying: "祝您……。"

① 生日快乐
HAPPY BIRTHDAY

② 身体健康
GOOD HEALTH

③ 节日快乐
HAPPY HOLIDAY

3. Start with a big piece of art paper. Create a year calendar for twelve months just like the one below.

You will go around the class to ask everyone's birthday. Indicate them in the boxes under the months. Next, look up the birth dates of at least two famous Chinese people and do the same exercise.

If today is someone's birthday, greet him/her saying "祝你生日快乐！"

一月 January	二月 February	三月 March	四月 April
十五号是王老师的生日	十三号是Steven的生日 二十二号是马克的生日	今天是二十一号，是John的生日！ 祝John生日快乐！	
五月 May	六月 June	七月 July	八月 August
		八号是玛丽的生日 十九号是Tom的生日 三十号是Jason的生日	
九月 September	十月 October	十一月 November	十二月 December
三号是Casey的生日 十二号是YaoMing的生日！			

Fun Time!

The Chinese lunar calendar does not accurately follow the seasons of the solar year. To assist farmers to decide when to plant or harvest crops, the Chinese list 24 seasonal markers, known as 节气 (jiēqi, solar term). The table below shows the 24 solar terms and the approximate Gregorian dates they correspond to.

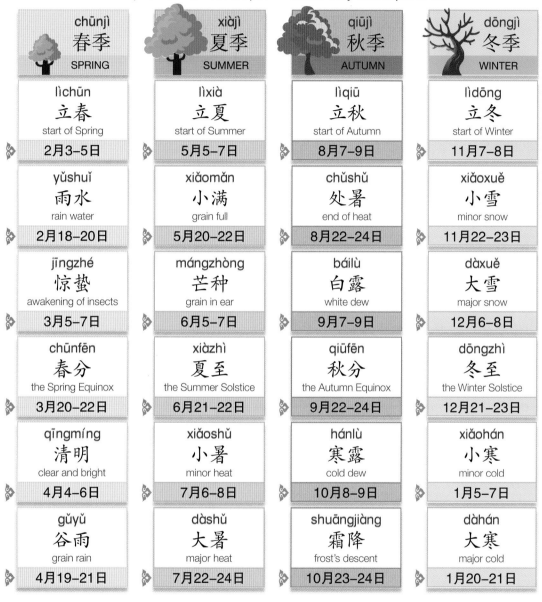

chūnjì 春季 SPRING	xiàjì 夏季 SUMMER	qiūjì 秋季 AUTUMN	dōngjì 冬季 WINTER
lìchūn 立春 start of Spring — 2月3–5日	lìxià 立夏 start of Summer — 5月5–7日	lìqiū 立秋 start of Autumn — 8月7–9日	lìdōng 立冬 start of Winter — 11月7–8日
yǔshuǐ 雨水 rain water — 2月18–20日	xiǎomǎn 小满 grain full — 5月20–22日	chǔshǔ 处暑 end of heat — 8月22–24日	xiǎoxuě 小雪 minor snow — 11月22–23日
jīngzhé 惊蛰 awakening of insects — 3月5–7日	mángzhòng 芒种 grain in ear — 6月5–7日	báilù 白露 white dew — 9月7–9日	dàxuě 大雪 major snow — 12月6–8日
chūnfēn 春分 the Spring Equinox — 3月20–22日	xiàzhì 夏至 the Summer Solstice — 6月21–22日	qiūfēn 秋分 the Autumn Equinox — 9月22–24日	dōngzhì 冬至 the Winter Solstice — 12月21–23日
qīngmíng 清明 clear and bright — 4月4–6日	xiǎoshǔ 小暑 minor heat — 7月6–8日	hánlù 寒露 cold dew — 10月8–9日	xiǎohán 小寒 minor cold — 1月5–7日
gǔyǔ 谷雨 grain rain — 4月19–21日	dàshǔ 大暑 major heat — 7月22–24日	shuāngjiàng 霜降 frost's descent — 10月23–24日	dàhán 大寒 major cold — 1月20–21日

The following is a poem on the 24 solar terms. It contains a word from each of the 24 solar terms. List them out and then read the poem aloud with your teacher.

二十四节气歌(gē)

chūn yǔ jīng chūn qīng gǔ tiān, xià mǎn máng xià shǔ xiāng lián,
春 雨 惊 春 清 谷 天, 夏 满 芒 夏 暑 相 连,

qiū chǔ lù qiū hán shuāng jiàng, dōng xuě xuě dōng xiǎo dà hán
秋 处 露 秋 寒 霜 降, 冬 雪 雪 冬 小 大 寒

I have learned...

Core Vocabulary

年 n.		nián	year	多大 phr.			duō dà	how old
今年 n.		jīnnián	this year	个 m.w.	個		gè	*(used for months, weeks, people, etc.)*
明年 n.		míngnián	next year	上个月 phr.	上個月		shàng gè yuè	last month
去年 n.		qùnián	last year	这 pron.	這		zhè/zhèi	this
前年 n.		qiánnián	the year before last	这个月 phr.	這個月		zhè/zhèi gè yuè	this month
后年 n.		hòunián	the year after next	下个月 phr.	下個月		xià gè yuè	next month
月 n.		yuè	month; moon	这个星期 phr.	這個星期		zhè/zhèi gè xīngqī	this week
号 n.	號	hào	number; date *(spoken Chinese)*	上个星期 phr.	上個星期		shàng gè xīngqī	last week
日 n.		rì	day; date *(written Chinese)*	下个星期 phr.	下個星期		xià gè xīngqī	next week
前天 n.		qiántiān	the day before yesterday	年纪 n.	年紀		niánjì	age
后天 n.		hòutiān	the day after tomorrow	呢 part.			ne	*(used to form questions)*
星期 n.		xīngqī	week	祝 v.			zhù	wish
的 part.		de	*(used after an attributive)*	快乐 adj.	快樂		kuàilè	happy; joyful
生日 n.		shēngrì	birthday	节日 n.	節日		jiérì	holiday; festival
岁 n.	歲	suì	year of age					

Extended Vocabulary

周 n.	週	zhōu	week	一路平安 phr.		yílù píng'ān	bon voyage
新年 n.		Xīnnián	New Year	身体 n.		shēntǐ	body; health
周末 n.	週末	zhōumò	weekend	健康 n.		jiànkāng	good health
好运 phr.	好運	hǎo yùn	good luck				

今年是2011年。	明天星期六。	两个月；四个星期	你呢？/你的呢？
上个月是四月。	下个星期五是七号。	你多大？/你几岁？	祝你生日快乐！
今天二月五号。	三年；七天	我的生日是一月三号。	

I can do!

Interpretive **Communication**

❑ I can understand the date when it is told to me.

❑ I can understand when someone says his/her age.

❑ I can read dates in Chinese.

Interpersonal **Communication**

❑ I can exchange information about dates.

❑ I can ask someone's age and tell my age.

❑ I can talk about birthdays.

❑ I can express good wishes.

Presentational **Communication**

❑ I can tell people the year, month, day, and day of the week.

❑ I can tell what day it is (today, yesterday, tomorrow).

❑ I can talk about some Chinese festivals.

Cultural **Knowledge**

❑ I can compare the Chinese lunar calendar with the Gregorian calendar.

❑ I can explain how some Chinese words are related to early pictographs.

❑ I can ask a Chinese person his or her age in a culturally appropriate way.

❑ I can identify some Chinese festivals and holidays.

❑ I can state one or two names of the 24 solar terms and the appropriate Gregorian dates they correspond to.

Meet David's family ...

My family

我们一家人

COMMUNICATIVE GOALS
- Talking about one's family
- Stating the size of a family
- Talking about one's siblings
- Describing people

Cultural Knowledge
- Kinship in Chinese culture
- Terms of address in the Chinese family
- 口 — a reference to population
- Chinese genealogy

ā
"我爱我家！"
This is how you say "I love my family!" in Chinese.

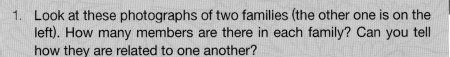
Get ready...

1. Look at these photographs of two families (the other one is on the left). How many members are there in each family? Can you tell how they are related to one another?

2. Next, compare your family with the families shown here, and complete the table below by filling in the numbers. Mark an X if a particular family member is not present.

... *and compare to* *Michelle's family.*

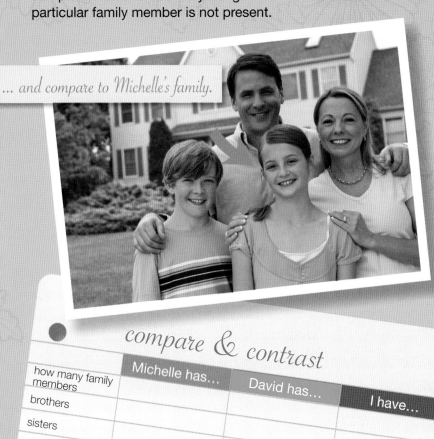

compare & contrast

how many family members	Michelle has...	David has...	I have...
brothers			
sisters			
are there others?			

127

STEP 1
ABOUT ONE'S FAMILY

这是谁？
Who is this?

1 这是我父亲。 *fùqīn*
This is my father.

那是谁？
Who is that?

2 那是我母亲。 *mǔqīn*
That is my mother.

A Introducing one's family

3 那是我姐姐。 *jiějie*
That is my older sister.

生词 NEW WORDS

父亲 n.	父親	fùqīn	father
哥哥 n.		gēge	older brother
姐姐 n.	jiějie	姊姊 zǐzi	older sister

母亲 n.	母親	mǔqīn	mother
弟弟 n.		dìdi	younger brother
妹妹 n.		mèimei	younger sister

LANGUAGE FOCUS

In Chinese, the formal way of saying "father" and "mother" is 父亲 and 母亲. In everyday conversations, it is common to say 爸爸 and 妈妈.

To ask who someone is, use 谁. Place it at the end of the question, right after 是.

Examples:

Question **Answer**

1 这是谁? 这是我哥哥。
Who is this? This is my older brother.

2 那是谁? 那是我妹妹。
Who is that? That is my younger sister.

As mentioned in Lesson 4, when the pronouns 你, 我, 他 or 她 function as attributives to qualify kinship terms, it is not necessary to use the possessive marker 的.

Examples: 我父亲，他弟弟

However, when other attributives such as names are used, 的 must be placed between the two nouns.

Examples: 马克的父亲
Mark's father

芳芳的母亲
Fangfang's mother

128
STEP UP WITH CHINESE • 成长

1. Imagine the people in the pictures are related to you or someone whom you know. Use them to practice the following speech pattern.

这是谁?

这是我父亲。

1. my father 2. my mother 3. me 4. my younger sister

5. Josh 6. my teacher 7. my older sister 8. Michelle

2. For more practice, bring in a picture (or draw a picture) of your family members, and introduce them by applying the speech pattern shown here:

这是……。

那是……。

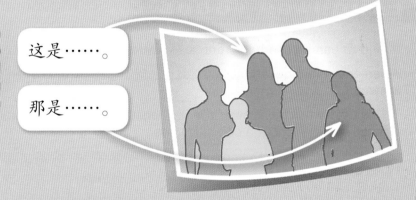

CULTURAL HIGHLIGHTS

Kinship in Chinese Culture

Traditionally, Chinese people value kinship very much. They are deeply attached to their family. Chinese parents are dedicated and concerned about their children's affairs throughout their lives. Their sons and daughters, in turn, are very respectful toward their parents.

Siblings show care and concern for one another by sharing very close ties, in the same way that the hands and feet of the body are interdependant. This is known as 手足之情 (shǒu zú zhī qíng). Chinese society places a high value on kinship and often evaluates a person's moral ethics by how much he/she cares for the family.

The modern Chinese family still holds kinship dear to their hearts.

这是你爸爸吗？
Is this your father?

对，这是我爸爸。
Yes, this is my father.

那是你妈妈吗？
Is that your mother?

不是，那是我阿姨。
No, that is my aunt.

LANGUAGE FOCUS

这 and 那 can be used as pronouns to refer to people.

When answering questions with "是……吗？", 对 or 是 is often used to make an affirmative answer.

不是 is used when the answer is in the negative. You may elaborate further by continuing with a negative statement or a corrective one.

Example: 不是，那不是我爸爸。那是我叔叔。

No, that is not my father.　　　　That is my uncle.

Practice the following dialogs with a classmate by referring to a family photo.

Student A: 　　　　　Student B:

❶ 这是你吗？　　　　对，这是我。

❷ 这是你爸爸吗？　　不是，这是我哥哥。

生 词 NEW WORDS

Paternal Line

爷爷 爺爺 yéye
paternal grandfather

奶奶 nǎinai
paternal grandmother

伯伯 bóbo
uncle, father's older
brother

爸爸

我

叔叔
uncle, father's younger
brother

姑姑 gūgu
aunt, father's sister

Maternal Line

外公 wàigōng
maternal grandfather

外婆 wàipó
maternal grandmother

妈妈

舅舅 jiùjiu
uncle, mother's brother

阿姨
aunt, mother's sister

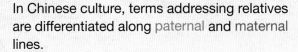

LANGUAGE FOCUS

In Chinese culture, terms addressing relatives are differentiated along paternal and maternal lines.

Examples:

爷爷
father's father

外公
mother's father

In addition, seniority amongst extended family members is also clearly differentiated.

Examples:

伯伯
father's older
brother

叔叔
father's younger
brother

Hence, once you understand this distinctively cultural structure, you can clearly identify one relative from the other.

Apply what you have learned thus far and put to practice the following examples:

Question	Answer
❶ 这是谁?	这是我奶奶。
❷ 那是谁?	那是我舅舅。
❸ 这是你叔叔吗?	对，这是我叔叔。
❹ 那是你阿姨吗?	不是，那是我姑姑。

1. Using the word bank provided, answer the following questions:

> 爷爷　叔叔　阿姨　外婆
> 姑姑　外公　奶奶　舅舅　伯伯

❶ 爸爸的爸爸是谁？　　❷ 爸爸的妈妈是谁？　　❸ 妈妈的爸爸是谁？

❹ 妈妈的妈妈是谁？　　❺ 爸爸的哥哥是谁？　　❻ 爸爸的弟弟是谁？

❼ 爸爸的姐姐是谁？　　❽ 妈妈的弟弟是谁？　　❾ 妈妈的妹妹是谁？

2. Look at three of your classmates' pictures showing their family and relatives. Take turns asking and answering questions about the people in the photo, using the speech pattern given. Then write down the responses in the chart below.

> Student A:
> 这是你叔叔吗？
>
> Student B:
> 对，这是我叔叔。/不是，这是我爸爸。

Names	Classmates' Family Members and Relatives
David	妈妈、姐姐、叔叔……

3. Create your own family tree and write down the relationships between you and your family members. You could also give their names, age and birthday. Then use the tree to introduce your family to the class.

For example, you can point to a man in the family tree and say:

> 他叫Michael，他是我叔叔。他35岁。
> 他的生日是3月5号。

你家有几口人？
kǒu

How many members are there in your family?

① 我家有五口人。

There are five members in my family.

A Stating the size of one's family

② 我家有六口人。

There are six members in my family.

NEW WORDS

生词

家² *n.*	jiā	family
有 *v.*	yǒu	have; possess
口 *m.w.*	kǒu	(used for members in the family)

² another meaning appeared in Lesson 2

LANGUAGE FOCUS

The verb 有 can be used to state the number of members a family has.

口 is a measure word for describing the number of members in a family. In Chinese, when asking about the number of people in one's family, the question phrase 几口人 is always used, even when there are more than 10 people in a family.

CULTURAL HIGHLIGHTS

口 — A Reference to Population

口, a pictograph from ancient times, vividly represents the word "mouth" and is closely related to the concept of family. Providing for one's family and bringing food to the table (or keeping the mouths fed) was probably the most important concern to a family in ancient China. So, when telling the number of family members, 口 is usually used as the measure word, for example, 三口人. When there's a new addition to a family, Chinese people would say, 我家多了(duō le)一口人 (*Lit.* There's one more mouth added to my family).

You will understand this term if you think in terms of a smaller human population, as in a family unit, and then extend that to a larger population, as in an entire country. It is in this way that 人口 refers to the population of a people or the number of mouths to feed.

1. Ask three of your classmates about his/her family using the speech pattern shown here:

Student A:
你家有几口人？

Student B:
我家有……口人。

2. Can you tell from the pictures or latest news how many members there are in each family? Work with a classmate and follow the speech pattern shown below.

Student A:
他/她家有几口人？

Student B:
他/她家有……口人。

(Year: 2007)

(Year: 2007)

(Year: 2008)

(Year: 2009)

(Year: 2010)

(Year: 2008)

爸爸、哥哥和我
Dad, brother and I

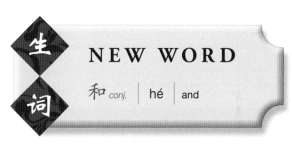

生词 | **NEW WORD**
和 *conj.* | hé | and

我和姐姐
My sister and I

LANGUAGE FOCUS

When talking about more than one person or object, the connecting word 和 is used. Read the following sentence:

我家有三口人：爸爸、妈妈和我。

As you can see, 和 is used between two nouns, but not between clauses or sentences.

Try This!

1. Practice the following dialog with a classmate.

   Student A: 你家有几口人？

   Student B: 我家有三口人：爸爸、妈妈和我。你家有几口人？

   Student A: 我家有六口人：爷爷、奶奶、爸爸、妈妈、弟弟和我。

2. Make a scrapbook of your family photos and add captions. In the captions use 和 as you list your family members.

My family photo scrapbook!

爸爸、妈妈、弟弟、妹妹和我。

STEP **3**
INTRODUCING ONE'S SIBLINGS

nánhái
一个男孩
One boy.

nǚhái
两个女孩
Two girls.

A Measure word for persons

生词

NEW WORDS

男孩 *n.*	nánhái	boy
女孩 *n.*	nǚhái	girl

LANGUAGE FOCUS

When quantifying a noun, there should be a measure word (between the number and the noun). Different nouns carry different measure words. 个 is a universal word that can replace most measure words. In this lesson, 个 is used with people.

Examples:
一个人，两个女孩，三个男孩

When introducing a person from an older generation or of a higher status, you may use 位 (wèi) instead of 个. However, it is incorrect to say 一位人.

Examples:
一位校长，两位老师

1. Look at the picture on the right and practice using 个 to express the number of people shown in total. Next, state the number of males and females.

2. Bring in a photo of a family and practice using 个 to express the number of family members in the photo.

Examples:
一个妹妹，两个……

136

yǒu

你有姐姐吗？ or

méi

你有没有姐姐？

Do you have an older sister?

我没有姐姐，

No I don't.

我有三个哥哥。

I have three older brothers.

生 词

NEW WORD

没有 v. | 没有 | méiyǒu | do not have

LANGUAGE FOCUS

When telling whether one has certain family members or relatives, we often use the verb 有. Its negative form is 没有.

Examples:

Questions	Answers
❶ 你有哥哥吗？ Do you have an older brother?	有。我有一个哥哥。 Yes, I have.
❷ 你有姐姐吗？ Do you have an older sister?	我没有姐姐。 No, I don't.

In addition to using "有……吗" structure to form a question, "有没有" can also be used to form the same question. In this case, it is not necessary to add 吗 at the end.

Examples:

Questions	Answers
❶ 你有没有弟弟？ Do you have a younger brother?	有。我有一个弟弟。 Yes, I have one younger brother.
❷ 你有没有妹妹？ Do you have a younger sister?	我没有妹妹。 No, I don't.

1. Use 有 or 没有 to answer the following questions.

❶ 你有哥哥吗?　　❷ 你有没有弟弟?

❸ 你有姐姐吗?　　❹ 你有没有妹妹?

2. Ask three of your classmates about their family information, then fill out the form below:

Examples:

你家有几口人?　你有哥哥吗?

你有没有姐姐?　你有几个弟弟?

名字	几口人	哥哥	姐姐	弟弟	妹妹
David	六口	一个	没有	没有	两个

138

DESCRIBING PEOPLE

生 词 NEW WORDS

| 头 | 頭 | tóu | head |

| 头发 | 頭髮 | tóufa | hair |

| 耳朵 | | ěrduo | ear | 鼻子 | bízi | nose |

| 眼睛 | yǎnjing | eye | 眉毛 | méimao | eyebrow |

| 嘴(巴) | zuǐ (ba) | mouth |

| 肩膀 | | jiānbǎng | shoulder |

| 胳膊 | | gēbo | arm |

| 手 | | shǒu | hand |

| 肚子 | dùzi | stomach |

A Head to toe in Chinese

| 腿 | | tuǐ | leg |

LANGUAGE FOCUS

To describe someone, it would be helpful to learn what each part of the body is called in Chinese.

Follow this pattern:

我 + 的 + *a body part*

Examples: 我的耳朵，我的鼻子

| 脚 | 腳 | jiǎo | foot |

1. Use the nouns you have learned above and practice by saying: "这是我的_____。"

2. Work in a team of four and take turns. The first member of the team will say the different parts of the body as quickly and fluently as a second classmate points to them. He or she has only 20 seconds to say all of the body parts correctly and no repetition is allowed. A third classmate will keep time, while a fourth classmate will keep score.

gāo

哥哥很高，

The older brother is tall,

ǎi

弟弟很矮。

the younger brother is short.

pàng

叔叔很胖，

The man is overweight,

shòu

阿姨很瘦。

the woman is slim.

NEW WORDS

高 adj.	gāo	tall
矮 adj.	ǎi	short
胖 adj.	pàng	fat
瘦 adj.	shòu	slim

生词

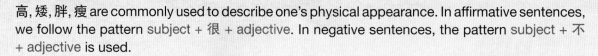

LANGUAGE FOCUS

高, 矮, 胖, 瘦 are commonly used to describe one's physical appearance. In affirmative sentences, we follow the pattern subject + 很 + adjective. In negative sentences, the pattern subject + 不 + adjective is used.

Consider the following examples:

Questions	Answers
❶ 你爸爸高吗？ Is your father tall?	我爸爸很高。 Yes, he is.
❷ 你哥哥胖吗？ Is your older brother overweight?	我哥哥不胖。 No, he's not.

Try This!

1. **Pair Work:** Find a family photo and let your partner ask and comment about the family members in the photo.

   Follow this dialog pattern and use clues from the word bank:

   高　矮　胖　瘦

   Student A:

   ❶ 这是你姐姐吗？

   ❷ 你妈妈很高。

   Student B:

   不是，这是我妈妈。

   对，她很高，也很瘦。

2. **Comprehension:** Read the following short passage and answer the questions.

   我叫李小芳，今年14岁。我家有四口人，爸爸、妈妈、哥哥和我。我爸爸今年42岁，他很高、不胖。我妈妈40岁，她不高，很瘦。我哥哥也很高，不胖不瘦，今年16岁。

   ❶ Who are tall in the family?
   a. 爸爸和妈妈　b. 爸爸和哥哥
   c. 哥哥和妈妈　d. 小芳和哥哥

   ❷ Who is very thin in the family?
   a. 爸爸　　　　b. 哥哥
   c. 妈妈　　　　d. 小芳

STEP 1
ABOUT ONE'S FAMILY

Looking at a photo, two friends are talking about family

这是谁?

　　这是我奶奶。

那是你爷爷吗?

　　不是，那是我外公。

你外公多大年纪?

　　八十八。

STEP 2
NUMBERS OF MEMBERS IN A FAMILY

The same two friends continue talking about the number of family members in each family

你家有几口人?

　　我家有三口人，爸爸、妈妈
　　和我。你家呢?

我家有七口人，爷爷、奶奶、
爸爸、妈妈、哥哥、姐姐和我。

　　你家人很多。

我们都很快乐。

STEP 3
INTRODUCING ONE'S SIBLINGS

A student asking another about his siblings

你有哥哥吗?

　　有。

你有几个哥哥?

　　我有两个哥哥。

你有弟弟吗?

　　没有，我有一个妹妹。

我也有一个妹妹。

STEP 4
DESCRIBING PEOPLE

Name the parts of the body in Chinese

头、头发、眉毛、眼睛、鼻子、
嘴巴、耳朵

肩膀、胳膊、手、肚子、腿、脚

A student describing his brother and grandmother

这是我哥哥。他很高，眼睛
很大。那是我奶奶。她不高
不矮、不胖不瘦，身体
很健康。

shēntǐ
body

Step Up!

1. Find or take a picture of your family. You can use one or many pictures. In Chinese, write the information of each member of your family below the picture. Put the pictures in your portfolio. Share the information with another student in the class.

name	relation	birthday	age	appearance
Lee Richards	父亲	一九七二年七月八日	三十九岁	他很高、不胖。

2. **Role play:** Divide into "family groups" of five students each. Every group is made up of a mother, father, grandmother, grandfather, and son or daughter. Each group presents itself to the class, with each group member introducing himself/herself using sentence patterns learned in this lesson.

   Example: 我是爸爸。我很高。我不矮。

3. **Who is it?** Take turns describing another student from the class, including gender, age and characteristics, without mentioning the other student's name. The rest of the class tries to guess the person being described.

   Example: 他是男孩。他很高。他不胖……

Fun Time!

Below is a genealogy from the Jia clan featured in the Chinese classic masterpiece *Dream of the Red Chamber*. Male and female names are marked in black and red respectively. Can you find the similarity between the names in each generation? Also, why is ★*Jia Baoyu* not named in the same way as his brothers and male cousins? Research to find out ...

Chinese Genealogy, known as 家谱 (jiāpǔ) is a written record of a clan's history and lineage. It documents the origins of the surname, the migration patterns of the clan, the family lineage, the ancestral biography, the story of the locality, etc. Interestingly, it also sets a naming system for descendants of the clan. For example, descendants belonging to the same generation share a <u>same character or radical</u> in their given names; the prescribed character or radical will be recycled after a few generations.

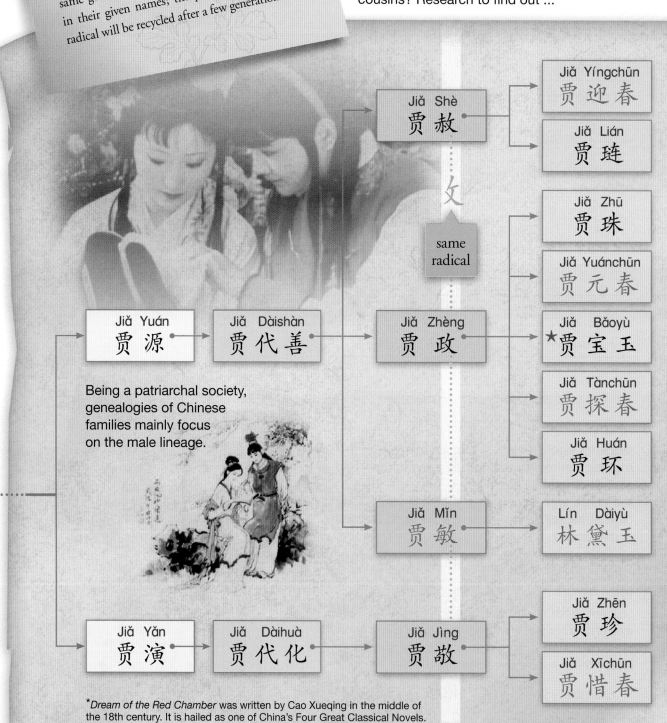

Being a patriarchal society, genealogies of Chinese families mainly focus on the male lineage.

Jiǎ Yuán 贾源 → Jiǎ Dàishàn 贾代善 → Jiǎ Zhèng 贾政

Jiǎ Shè 贾赦 → Jiǎ Yíngchūn 贾迎春 / Jiǎ Lián 贾琏

父 same radical

Jiǎ Zhèng 贾政 → Jiǎ Zhū 贾珠 / Jiǎ Yuánchūn 贾元春 / ★Jiǎ Bǎoyù 贾宝玉 / Jiǎ Tànchūn 贾探春 / Jiǎ Huán 贾环

Jiǎ Mǐn 贾敏 → Lín Dàiyù 林黛玉

Jiǎ Yǎn 贾演 → Jiǎ Dàihuà 贾代化 → Jiǎ Jìng 贾敬 → Jiǎ Zhēn 贾珍 / Jiǎ Xīchūn 贾惜春

Dream of the Red Chamber was written by Cao Xueqing in the middle of the 18th century. It is hailed as one of China's Four Great Classical Novels.

I have learned...

Core Vocabulary

父亲 n.	父親	fùqīn	father	男孩 n.		nánhái	boy
母亲 n.	母親	mǔqīn	mother	女孩 n.		nǔhái	girl
哥哥 n.		gēge	older brother	头 n.	頭	tóu	head
姐姐 n.	姊姊	jiějie/zǐzi	older sister	头发 n.	頭髮	tóufa	hair
弟弟 n.		dìdi	younger brother	眼睛 n.		yǎnjing	eye
妹妹 n.		mèimei	younger sister	耳朵 n.		ěrduo	ear
家² n.		jiā	home family	眉毛 n.		méimao	eyebrow
口 m.w.		kǒu	(used for members in the family)	鼻子 n.		bízi	nose
和 conj.		hé	and	嘴(巴) n.		zuǐ (ba)	mouth
有 v.		yǒu	have; possess	胳膊 n.		gēbo	arm
没有 v.	沒有	méiyou	do not have	肩膀 n.		jiānbǎng	shoulder
爷爷 n.	爺爺	yéye	paternal grandfather	肚子 n.		dùzi	stomach
奶奶 n.		nǎinai	paternal grandmother	手 n.		shǒu	hand
外公 n.		wàigōng	maternal grandfather	腿 n.		tuǐ	leg
外婆 n.		wàipó	maternal grandmother	脚 n.	腳	jiǎo	foot
伯伯 n.		bóbo	uncle, father's older brother	高 adj.		gāo	tall
叔叔 n.		shūshu	uncle, father's younger brother	矮 adj.		ǎi	short
姑姑 n.		gūgu	aunt, father's sister	胖 adj.		pàng	fat
舅舅 n.		jiùjiu	uncle, mother's brother	瘦 adj.		shòu	slim
阿姨 n.		āyí	aunt, mother's sister				

I have learned...

这是谁？这是我<u>父亲</u>。

那是谁？那是我<u>母亲</u>。

这是你爸爸吗？<u>对</u>，这是我爸爸。

那是你妈妈吗？<u>不是</u>，那是我<u>阿姨</u>。

你家有<u>几</u><u>口</u>人？我家有三<u>口</u>人。

爸爸、妈妈<u>和</u>我

一个男孩，两个女孩

你<u>有</u>哥哥吗？<u>有</u>。我有一个哥哥。

你<u>有没有</u>姐姐？我<u>没有</u>姐姐。

我的<u>头发</u>。我的<u>耳朵</u>。

我姐姐很<u>高</u>。

我弟弟很<u>胖</u>。

146

I can do!

Interpretive Communication

❑ I can understand the family titles used to refer to a member of the family.

❑ I can understand descriptive words for a person.

❑ I can understand when someone introduces their immediate family members.

❑ I can understand when my classmates and others introduce their relatives.

Interpersonal Communication

❑ I can exchange information about family members with classmates and others.

❑ I can ask and answer questions about how many members there are in a family.

❑ I can exchange descriptive details about a person's appearance with my classmates and others.

Presentational Communication

❑ I can tell people about my family.

❑ I can introduce my other relatives.

❑ I can describe my family members.

❑ I can tell basic descriptive details about a person.

Cultural Knowledge

❑ I can understand the importance of kinship in Chinese culture.

❑ I can use Chinese terms of address for family members correctly.

❑ I can explain how the word 口 (mouth) is used to refer to the human population.

❑ I can state the naming pattern in Chinese genealogies.

My family pet

我家的宠物

COMMUNICATIVE GOALS

• Identifying animals in Chinese
• Expressing likes and dislikes for animals
• Talking about animals and pets
• Describing how animals move

Cultural Knowledge

• Pets in China and other countries
• The giant panda
• The Chinese dragon and phoenix
• Beijing Zoo and the National Zoo of U.S.A.
• The 12 zodiac animals

Get ready...

Global Connection: To many people around the world, pets are regarded as members of the family, and share close relationship with their owners. Take a look at the chart below on world statistics for the numbers of pets in various countries. What impressions can you gather from the statistics? Try answering these questions:

1. Which countries have the largest numbers of dogs, cats, birds and fish as pets?
2. What is the most popular pet in each country?
3. Why do you think there are more fish than other pets in all countries listed here?

World Statistics	Dog	Cat	Bird	Fish
Australia	3,700,000	2,200,000	7,100,000	12,900,000
China	22,908,000	53,100,000	71,474,000	121,852,000
France	8,150,000	9,600,000	6,500,000	28,000,000
Italy	7,600,000	9,400,000	13,000,000	30,000,000
Japan	9,650,000	7,300,000	21,300,000	34,100,000
U.S.A.	61,080,000	76,420,000	18,740,000	168,990,000

Source: www.mapsofworld.com/world-top-ten (Year: 2008-09)

STEPS *at a glance!*

STEP 1

TYPES OF ANIMALS

A. Domestic and farm animals
这是什么动物?
这是狗。

B. At the zoo . . .
动物园有熊猫，还有狮子。

STEP 2

EXPRESSING LIKES AND DISLIKES

A. Animals I like and dislike
你喜欢不喜欢小狗?
我喜欢小狗。

B. Giving additional information
我喜欢小狗，也喜欢小猫。

C. Animals I like most or least
我最不喜欢蛇。

STEP 3

COUNTING ANIMALS

A. Measure words for animals
一只小狗、两条蛇、
三头牛、四匹马

B. Telling the number of family pets
你家有没有小狗?
有，我家有一只小狗。

STEP 4

HOW ANIMALS MOVE

小鸟飞、兔子跳

生 词 NEW WORDS

dòngwù
这(那)是什么动物*?
What animal is this (that)?

māo　　　　gǒu
这是猫。　那是狗。
This is a cat.　That is a dog.

* 動物
　寵物

A Domestic and farm animals

tā
它叫猫猫。
It (She) is called Maomao.

它叫狗狗。
It (He) is called Gougou.

chǒngwù
它们都是我家的宠物*。
They are both my (family) pets.

yú	jī	zhū	niǎo	yáng	niú	mǎ	tùzi
鱼 魚	鸡 鷄	猪 豬	鸟 鳥	羊	牛	马 馬	兔子
fish	chicken	pig	bird	sheep, goat	ox, cow	horse	rabbit

LANGUAGE FOCUS

As you have learned in Lessons 1 and 2, 什么 is used to ask "what" questions. It is placed at the end of a sentence (e.g. 这是什么?) or before a noun (e.g. 这是什么动物?). To answer the question, simply retain the word order and replace 什么 with the required information.

Note that when referring to a person, we use the pronoun 他/她 for "him/her." 它, singular, or 它们, plural, are the pronouns to use when referring to animals and objects.

1. Use these flash cards depicting different animals to practice dialogs with your partner. Follow the speech patterns shown below:

1
这是什么动物？
这是……。

狗

鸟

猫

鱼

兔子

2
那是什么动物？
那是……。

鸡

羊

马

猪

牛

2. Bring pictures of your pets or pets of your relatives or neighbor and introduce them using the following speech pattern:

这是……。 它叫……。 它……岁。

 CULTURAL HIGHLIGHTS

Pets in China

Raising pets in China has a long historical tradition. Keeping and admiring flowers, birds, insects and fish are traditional leisure activities that Chinese engage in. Chinese people have always had a wide range of interest in animals, ranging from birds and crickets to dogs and cats.

Every day when dusk falls, there are often people walking in the streets of Beijing with little animals running in front of or behind them. These animals are their family pets.

Influenced by life in the imperial court, keeping birds was once common in old Beijing. In the past, even non-aristocrats in Beijing kept birds. In the early morning, people could be seen everywhere in the parks "walking" their birds (遛鸟 liù niǎo).

dòngwùyuán
动物园*有什么动物？
What animals are there at the zoo?

xióngmāo　　hái　　shīzi
动物园有熊猫，还*有狮子*。
There are pandas. There are also lions at the zoo.

*动物園
還
獅子

lǎohǔ
老虎
tiger

hóuzi
猴子
monkey

shé
蛇
snake

LANGUAGE FOCUS

In Chinese 还 is used to provide more details on the same topic. To use 还 in a sentence, place it before the second verb.

❶ 我家有小狗，还有小猫。
Our family has a dog. We also have a cat.

❷ 芳芳有小鸟，还有小鱼。
Fangfang has a bird. She also has a fish.

还 can also be used to ask for more details on the same topic. To answer such questions, your reply should also contain 还. Look at the following dialog:

动物园有什么动物？
动物园有大熊猫。

还有什么动物？ What *else* (other animals) are there?
还有猴子。 There are monkeys too.

1. Use 还 to answer the following questions. Follow the speech patterns shown below to answer each question:

❶ What animals are there at the zoo?

> 动物园有……，还有……。

❷ What pets are popular in China?

> 中国有……，还有……。

❸ Do you have any siblings?

> 我有……，还有……。

❹ What pets are popular in the U.S.A.?

> 美国有……，还有……。

2. Do a research on the most popular animals found in the national zoos of U.S.A. and China. Make a list of your findings and share them with your classmates by practice saying the speech patterns shown below. Also, try saying the Chinese names of the animals if you know them. If you don't, ask your teacher or find out on the Internet.

> 美国动物园有……，还有……。

> 中国动物园有……，还有……。

CULTURAL HIGHLIGHTS

The Giant Panda

Giant pandas are precious animals in China. They live in a few mountain ranges in central China, in particular the provinces of Sichuan, Shaanxi, and Gansu. The China Conservation and Research Center for the Giant Panda in Sichuan's Wolong is home to many giant pandas.

There are about 1,600 giant pandas left in the wild, and they are listed as an endangered species. More than 160 pandas live in zoos and breeding centers around the world, mostly in China.

Giant pandas first came to the National Zoo in Washington, D.C. in 1972, shortly after President Nixon visited China. Other zoos in the United States that have giant pandas include the San Diego Zoo, the Atlanta Zoo, and the Memphis Zoo. China has sent giant pandas to zoos in a number of other countries as well, making them both cultural icons and ambassadors of China.

xǐhuan
你喜欢宠物吗？
Do you like pets?

我喜欢宠物。
Yes, I like pets.

A Animals I like and dislike

你喜欢不喜欢蛇？
Do you like snakes?

我不喜欢蛇。
No, I don't like snakes.

生 词
NEW WORDS

| 喜欢 v. | 喜歡 | xǐhuan | like |

LANGUAGE FOCUS

The verb 喜欢 is used to express one's likes. To ask about one's likes, either of the two question patterns "喜欢……吗" or "喜欢不喜欢" can be used. 喜欢不喜欢 follows the structure verb + 不 + verb.

Examples:

❶ 你是不是小伟? Are you Xiaowei (or not)?

❷ 你姓不姓王? Is your last name Wang (or not)?

In everyday conversations, 喜欢不喜欢 is usually simplified to 喜不喜欢.

To express one's dislikes, simply add 不 before 喜欢.

Examples:

❶ 我不喜欢宠物。

❷ 我不喜欢蛇。

Try This!

Work with a partner. Ask each other questions about pets using 喜欢. Share your partner's answers with the class.

Examples:　❶ 你喜欢宠物吗?（你喜欢不喜欢宠物?）
❷ 你喜欢什么宠物?
❸ 你的爸爸妈妈喜欢不喜欢宠物?（哥哥、姐姐、弟弟、妹妹）
❹ 他们喜欢什么宠物?

我喜欢狗，
也喜欢猫。

I like dogs; I like cats too.

我不喜欢蛇，
他也不喜欢蛇。

I don't like snakes. Neither does he.

LANGUAGE FOCUS

Here, the adverb 也 has the same meaning "also" as was first introduced in Lesson 2 (我也是美国人). It can be placed before a second verb phrase to give additional information about the subject.

Example:

爸爸喜欢鸟，也喜欢鱼。

It can also be used to indicate that two different subjects share similar properties or perform the same action.

Example:

我喜欢猫，她也喜欢猫。

In the negative, 也 is placed before the second 不 in the sentence.

Examples:

❶ 我不喜欢蛇，也不喜欢老虎。
❷ 我不喜欢蛇，她也不喜欢蛇。

1. Read the dialog in the right column and answer the questions below:

❶ A 喜欢什么宠物？
❷ B 喜欢什么宠物？
❸ 谁喜欢狗和猫？

A: 你喜欢宠物吗？
B: 很喜欢。你呢？
A: 我也很喜欢。你喜欢什么宠物？
B: 我喜欢狗。你呢？
A: 我也喜欢狗。你喜欢猫吗？
B: 喜欢。我喜欢狗，也喜欢猫。

2. Use this dialog as a model and create a similar one with a partner. See the following conversation:

Student A:

❶ 你喜欢什么动物？
❷ 你喜欢不喜欢老虎？

Student B:

我喜欢熊猫，也喜欢狮子。
我不喜欢老虎，也不喜欢蛇。

C Animals I like most or least

zuì
我 最 喜 欢 蛇。
I like snakes most.

我 最 不 喜 欢 蛇。
I dislike snakes most.

生 词

NEW WORD

最 *adv.* | zuì | most

LANGUAGE FOCUS

最 is an adverb that tells us about the intensity or degree of an action or adjective. To talk about the animals you like most or least, place 最 before the verb to form the pattern 最 + verb (affirmative) or 最 + 不 + verb (negative).

Try This!

Make three sets of flash cards containing the following:

Set 1: People (我, 妈妈, 哥哥, 爸爸, 朋友……)
Set 2: Adverbs (很, 不, 也, 最)
Set 3: Animals (小猫, 小鱼, 熊猫, 兔子……)

Put each set of cards in a different stack. Next, ask your classmates to take turns to pick out a card from each stack. Your classmates will use the words appearing on three cards to make a sentence with 喜欢 (see below), and read aloud the complete sentence to the class.

Example:

STEP 3

COUNTING ANIMALS

A Measure words for animals

As mentioned in Lesson 4, measure words are usually required when counting nouns, for example, 三个月，四个星期. When counting animals, the following measure words are used.

NEW WORDS 生 词

zhī

只
隻

一只猫   两只兔子

(Used for most animals)

tiáo

条
條

一条蛇   一条鱼

(Used mainly for animals with long bodies)

两头牛

tóu

头
頭

三头狮子

(Used for large animals)

一匹马

pǐ

匹

(Used mainly for horses)

Try This!

1. Match the animal to the correct measure word.

| 只 | 条 | 头 | 匹 |

❶ 鸟   ❷ 猴子   ❸ 鸡   ❹ 牛   ❺ 鱼   ❻ 马   ❼ 狮子   ❽ 熊猫

2. Rearrange the words to form sentences.

❶ 八条 / 有 / 鱼 / 马克
❷ 有 / 安琪 / 小猫 / 两只
❸ 一只 / 兔子 / 芳芳 / 有

❹ 叔叔 / 马 / 有 / 一匹
❺ 牛 / 大卫 / 两头 / 有
❻ 我 / 狗 / 有 / 三只

157

3. Use the correct measure word to tell your partner the number of animals in each picture.

五条鱼!

 ①  ②  ③  ④  ⑤

 ⑥  ⑦  ⑧  ⑨  ⑩

B Telling the number of family pets

你家有狗吗?
　有，我家有一只狗。
Do you have a dog (at home)? Yes, I have one.

你家有没有猫?
　没有，我家没有猫。
Do you have a cat (at home)? No, I don't.

LANGUAGE FOCUS

Similar to asking about one's siblings "你有姐姐吗? 你有没有哥哥? " (Lesson 5), the structure "有……吗" or "有没有" can also be used to ask about the pets in one's family.

When answering such a question, the number of pets can be mentioned. Note that the measure word must be used together with the numbers.

For negative answers, there is no need to include the number of pets.

Try This!

Interview your classmates to find out if they have any pets at home. If yes, ask "how many?" and make a record. Also ask for the pet's name. Follow the speech pattern below. Record your findings in Chinese.

你家有没有宠物？ 有几只？ 叫什么名字？

姓名	你有没有宠物？	有几只狗？	有几只猫？	有几只鸟？	有几条鱼？	qítā 其他 others
马克	有	两只狗 Ringo, Sam	没有猫	一只鸟 Ricky	两条鱼 nameless	没有

LESSON 6 MY FAMILY PET

STEP 4
HOW ANIMALS MOVE

Animals move about differently. To describe how the animals move, place each action verb after the animal's name.

fēi
小鸟飞 飛
fly

yóu
小鱼游
swim

pǎo
小狗跑
run

生 词 NEW WORDS

tiào
兔子跳
jump

wūguī   pá
乌龟爬
tortoise   crawl(s)

Try This!

1. Below is an interesting rhyme about the movements of various animals. Read it out loud and share its meaning in English with the class.

小狗跑，小猫跳，乌龟爬，鸟儿飞。

小鱼、小鱼，你在哪儿？

shuō
小鱼说我不跑，我不跳，我不爬也不飞。

shuǐ   lái qù zhēn
我在水中游，游来游去，真快乐。

2. Fill in the blanks with the appropriate action verb from the word bank. Then read it aloud to your partner.

飞　游　跑　跳　爬

❶ 牛＿＿＿＿＿＿＿＿＿＿＿＿＿。

❷ 小鸟＿＿＿＿＿＿＿＿＿＿＿＿。

❸ 小鱼＿＿＿＿＿＿＿＿＿＿＿＿。

❹ 兔子＿＿＿＿＿＿＿＿＿＿＿＿。

❺ 蛇＿＿＿＿＿＿＿＿＿＿＿＿＿。

❻ 小猫＿＿＿＿＿＿＿＿＿＿＿＿。

❼ 马＿＿＿＿＿＿＿＿＿＿＿＿＿。

❽ 猴子＿＿＿＿＿＿＿＿＿＿＿＿。

❾ 鸡＿＿＿＿＿＿＿＿＿＿＿＿＿。

❿ 狮子＿＿＿＿＿＿＿＿＿＿＿＿。

3. Divide into two groups. A member from Group A will mimic certain actions. Group B will guess what the action is and say it out in Chinese. After a few rounds, switch roles so that members in Group B will mimic the actions and Group A will guess.

Guess what action
I am doing?

The Dragon Soars and the Phoenix Dances

lóng　fèng wǔ
龙飞凤舞

龙 stands for the dragon, and 凤 for the phoenix. Both are legendary creatures in Chinese culture.

In contrast to the European dragon that is considered evil, the Chinese dragon is usually seen as benevolent with auspicious powers. The Chinese phoenix, gloriously beautiful, reigns over the feathered world in the legend.

The dragon is particularly popular in China and was a symbol of the Chinese emperor, with the phoenix being the symbol of the Chinese empresses. They are the principal motifs for decorative designs on buildings, clothing and articles of daily use in the imperial palace.

The action word 飞 aptly portrays the dragon soaring freely without restraint in the sky, while 舞 (dance) vividly describes the elegant moves of the phoenix.

STEP 1
TYPES OF ANIMALS

Two friends chatting at the entrance of a zoo

这个动物园有什么动物?
　　有老虎、狮子。
还有什么?
　　还有猴子。
那是什么动物?
　　那是大熊猫。
大熊猫很可爱!

kěài
lovable

STEP 2
EXPRESSING LIKES AND DISLIKES

Two friends talking about the pets they keep

你喜不喜欢宠物?
　　喜欢,很喜欢。你呢?
我也喜欢。我们一家人都喜欢宠物。
　　你家有什么宠物?
我家有猫、狗、鸟和鱼。
　　你最喜欢什么宠物?
我最喜欢猫。我妈妈最喜欢狗。
　　你爸爸呢?
我爸爸最喜欢鱼。
　　我爸爸也很喜欢鱼。

STEP 3
COUNTING ANIMALS

Two students describing the numbers of pets they have

你家有没有宠物?
　　有,我家有两只小狗。你家也有宠物吗?
有,有很多。我家有一只小猫、两只兔子、八条鱼。
　　你最喜欢什么宠物?
我都喜欢!

STEP 4
HOW ANIMALS MOVE

Note the action verbs that describe different movements of various animals

飞:鸟 (龙、凤)
游:鱼
跑:老虎、狮子、马
跳:兔子、猴子、小猫
爬:乌龟、蛇

1. **Group Work:** Below is a zoo map. Plan an imaginary trip to visit the various animals. Decide which animals you will see first, then second, third, etc. Pair up with another student and tell him/her about your trip.

Step Up!

When in doubt, follow speech pattern 1, ask your teacher the names of these animals in Chinese. Next, make a record of these animal names on your own. Then, practice speech pattern 2. Read aloud and act as though you are actually at the zoo.

Animal	动物	Pinyin
		xióngmāo
panda	熊猫	shīzi
lion	狮子	

❶ 老师，这是什么动物？

这是……。

那是什么动物？

那是……。

❷ 这个动物园有什么动物？

这个动物园有猴子、狮子和大熊猫，还有……、……和……。这个动物园也有……、……和……。

2. Create a four-page book in Chinese about your pet or imaginary pet. Include details such as its name, its birthday, its "family" members and their names, and what it likes or dislikes. Each page should have a picture and at least one sentence. You may draw pictures or use photographs.

它叫 Pancho。

它今年五岁，生日是三月二日。

它有一个姐姐，叫 Vivi。

我喜欢 Pancho，也喜欢 Vivi。

shēngxiào

十二生肖

The 12 Zodiac Animals

The Chinese zodiac, 十二生肖, consisting of twelve animals, is an important and interesting part of Chinese culture. It relates each year to an animal and its reputed attributes and follows a 12-year cycle. In China, everyone knows the animal sign of the year in which they were born, and it is a common topic of conversation.

To find your Chinese animal sign, just look up the year you were born on the chart below. For example, if you were born in 1998, your zodiac animal sign is a tiger.

To ask and answer questions about one's zodiac sign, follow the speech pattern below:

shǔ

Ⓐ 你属什么？

In which year were you born?

chūshēng

Ⓑ 我1998年出生，我属虎。

I was born in 1998, the year of the Tiger.

鼠 shǔ Rat

1900 1912 1924
1936 1948 1960
1972 1984 1996

牛 niú Ox

1901 1913 1925
1937 1949 1961
1973 1985 1997

虎 hǔ Tiger

1902 1914 1926
1938 1950 1962
1974 1986 1998

兔 tù Rabbit

1903 1915 1927
1939 1951 1963
1975 1987 1999

龙 lóng Dragon

1904 1916 1928
1940 1952 1964
1976 1988 2000

蛇 shé Snake

1905 1917 1929
1941 1953 1965
1977 1989 2001

马 mǎ Horse

1906 1918 1930
1942 1954 1966
1978 1990 2002

羊 yáng Goat

1907 1919 1931
1943 1955 1967
1979 1991 2003

猴 hóu Monkey

1908 1920 1932
1944 1956 1968
1980 1992 2004

鸡 jī Rooster

1909 1921 1933
1945 1957 1969
1981 1993 2005

狗 gǒu Dog

1910 1922 1934
1946 1958 1970
1982 1994 2006

猪 zhū Pig

1911 1923 1935
1947 1959 1971
1983 1995 2007

I have learned...

Core Vocabulary

猫 n.	貓	māo	cat		宠物 n.	寵物	chǒngwù	pet
狗 n.		gǒu	dog		动物 n.	動物	dòngwù	animal
鱼 n.	魚	yú	fish		动物园 n.	動物園	dòngwùyuán	zoo
马 n.	馬	mǎ	horse		还 adv.	還	hái	in addition (to), also
牛 n.		niú	cow, ox		最 adv.		zuì	most
羊 n.		yáng	sheep, goat		喜欢 v.	喜歡	xǐhuan	like
鸡 n.	雞	jī	chicken		只 m.w.	隻	zhī	(used for most animals)
猪 n.	豬	zhū	pig		条 m.w.	條	tiáo	(used mainly for animals with long bodies)
兔子 n.		tùzi	rabbit		头 m.w.	頭	tóu	(used for large animals, e.g. ox, pig)
猴子 n.		hóuzi	monkey		匹 m.w.		pǐ	(used mainly for horses)
熊猫 n.	熊貓	xióngmāo	panda		飞 v.	飛	fēi	fly
鸟 n.	鳥	niǎo	bird		跑 v.		pǎo	run
老虎 n.		lǎohǔ	tiger		跳 v.		tiào	jump
狮子 n.	獅子	shīzi	lion		爬 v.		pá	crawl, climb
蛇 n.		shé	snake		游 v.		yóu	swim

Extended Vocabulary

它 pron.		tā	it		属 v.	屬	shǔ	be born in the year of
龙 n.	龍	lóng	dragon		出生 v.		chūshēng	be born
凤 n.	鳳	fèng	phoenix		鼠 n.		shǔ	rat
舞 v.		wǔ	dance		乌龟 n.	烏龜	wūguī	tortoise

I have learned...

  SENTENCE PATTERNS

这是什么动物？这是狗。

动物园有熊猫，还有狮子。

你喜欢不喜欢小狗？我喜欢小狗。

我喜欢小狗，也喜欢小猫。

我最不喜欢蛇。

一只小狗、一条蛇、六头猪、两匹马

你家有狗吗？有，我家有一只狗。

你家有没有猫？没有，我家没有猫。

小鸟飞、小鱼游、小狗跑、乌龟爬、兔子跳

I can do!

Interpretive Communication

❑ I can identify common domestic, farm and zoo animals in Chinese.

❑ I can understand when someone expresses likes and dislikes for different animals.

❑ I can understand when someone expresses what he or she likes the most or least.

❑ I can read the characters of common domestic, farm and zoo animals.

Interpersonal Communication

❑ I can exchange information about my pets with others.

❑ I can ask and answer questions about someone's likes and dislikes.

❑ I can exchange information about the number of pets someone has.

Presentational Communication

❑ I can state different types of pets.

❑ I can introduce different types of pets.

❑ I can state the number of animals with the correct measure words.

❑ I can write a simple description about the pets I have.

Cultural Knowledge

❑ I can name and describe common pets in China and other countries.

❑ I can talk about the giant pandas and where they live.

❑ I can state some popular animals found in the zoos of China and U.S.A.

❑ I can state my Chinese zodiac animal sign and the other zodiac animal signs.

My school

我的学校

COMMUNICATIVE GOALS
- Introducing school facilities
- Describing locations
- Describing classroom items and their colors
- Talking about school courses

Cultural Knowledge
- Educational systems in China and the United States
- Classroom system in China
- China's National College Entrance Examination

Get ready...

Global Connection: Educational Systems

Education is a priority in many countries, and each has its own system that takes into account its local needs and culture. Below is a table showing how educational systems are organized in China and the U.S.A. Study it and answer the following questions:

1. What similarities and differences can you see in the educational systems of both countries?
2. Do you know of another educational system that is different from these two countries?
3. Education is compulsory in both countries. Can you work out the minimum number of years for general education in each country? Explain your answers.

STEP 1

DESCRIBING ONE'S SCHOOL

A. Describing the facilities in school
学校里有什么?
学校里有教学楼。
教学楼外有什么?
教学楼外有操场。

B. Specifying relative locations
图书馆在哪儿?
图书馆在教学楼(的)后边。

C. Telling how far one place is from another
你家离学校远吗?
我家离学校很远。

STEP 2

DESCRIBING ONE'S CLASSROOM

A. Things in a classroom
墙上有什么?
墙上有白板和钟。

B. Things in one's backpack
我有一个红色的书包。

C. Borrowing from friends
借我一支笔,行吗?
行,给你。

STEP 3

TALKING ABOUT COURSES AND CLASSES

A. Listing the courses one is taking
你有什么课?
我有中文课。

B. Number of courses/classes
你有几门课?
我有八门课。

C. Telling what courses one has taken
你学过生物吗?
我学过生物。

CHINA	
Level/Grade	Age
Primary	
1	6 – 7
2	7 – 8
3	8 – 9
4	9 – 10
5	10 – 11
6	11 – 12
Junior High	
7	12 – 13
8	13 – 14
9	14 – 15
Senior High	
10	15 – 16
11	16 – 17
12	17 – 18

U.S.A.	
Level/Grade	Age
Elementary	
Kindergarten	5 – 6
1	6 – 7
2	7 – 8
3	8 – 9
4	9 – 10
5	10 – 11
Middle	
6	11 – 12
7	12 – 13
8	13 – 14
High	
9 (Freshman)	14 – 15
10 (Sophomore)	15 – 16
11 (Junior)	16 – 17
12 (Senior)	17 – 18

xuéxiào
学 校
學 校
school

生 词 NEW WORDS

jiàoxuélóu
教 学 楼
教 學 樓
school building
(where classes are held)

jiàoshì
教 室
classroom

túshūguǎn
图 书 馆
圖 書 館
library

tǐyùguǎn
体 育 馆
體 育 館
gymnasium

cāochǎng
操 场
操 場
sports field

diànnǎoshì
电 脑 室
電 腦 室
computer room

cāntīng
餐 厅
cafeteria

yīwùshì
医 务 室
醫 務 室
medical room

A Describing the facilities in school

lǐ (bian)
学 校 里 (边) 有 什 么?
What's inside the school?

① 学 校 里 (边) 有 教 学 楼, 有 图 书 馆, 还 有 体 育 馆。
There is a school building, a library, and a gymnasium.
jiàoxuélóu　　túshūguǎn　　tǐyùguǎn

wài
教学楼外(边)有什么?
What's outside the school building?

cāochǎng
② 教学楼外(边)有操场。
Outside the school building is a sports field.

生 词

NEW WORDS

| 里(边)ₙ | 裏(邊) | lǐ (bian) | inside |
| 外(边)ₙ | 外(邊) | wài (bian) | outside |

LANGUAGE FOCUS

里 and 外 are directional words meaning "inside" and "outside," respectively. To refer to a specific location inside or outside a certain place, put the directional word after the name of the place. It is optional to attach the suffix 边 (or 面 miàn) to the directional word.

> *Examples:* ❶ 学校里 (in the school) ❷ 图书馆外 (outside the library)

Similar to the sentence "动物园有什么动物?" in Lesson 6, the phrase 有什么 is also used to ask about things in a place in this lesson. By attaching the directional words 里 and 外 to the place name, the location becomes more specific. When replying to such a question, you may use the structure "有……,有……,还有……" if you want to list a few things.

> *Examples:* ❶ 教学楼里有什么?
> What's inside the school building?
>
> ❷ 教学楼里有教室。
> There are classrooms inside the school building.
>
> *Or* ❸ 教学楼里有教室,有电脑室,还有医务室。
> Inside the school building are classrooms, computer rooms and a medical room.

Work with a classmate to ask and answer at least five questions about the school facilities. Make use of the directional words 里 and 外, as well as the question pattern "……有什么?"

To refresh your memory and reinforce what you have learned in Lessons 5 and 6, you may use the question pattern "有……吗?" or "有没有?" to ask yes-no questions about the school facilities.

> *Examples:*
>
> ❶ 学校里有什么?
> ❷ 学校里有餐厅吗?
> ❸ 学校里有没有体育馆?

School Map

生 词 NEW WORDS

图书馆

hòubian
后 边 *n.*
後 邊
behind

体育馆

北
西 东
南

zuǒbian
左 边 *n.*
左 邊
on the left

教学楼

餐厅

yòubian
右 边 *n.*
右 邊
on the right

医务室

zhōngjiān
中 间 *n.*
中 間
in the middle

pángbiān
旁 边 *n.*
旁 邊
beside

操场

qiānbian
前 边 *n.*
前 邊
in the front

When directional words such as 左, 右, 前, 后 are used with the suffix 边, they form position words that help us describe the location of people, places and things (e.g. 前边 means "in the front," 左边 means "on the left"). The suffix 边 here may be used interchangeably with the word 面 (e.g. 前面 is equivalent to 前边).

The word 在 is used as a verb meaning "be at, be in" in the following examples.

Examples:	**Question**	**Answer**
❶	图书馆在哪儿? Where is the library?	图书馆在教学楼(的)后边。 The library is behind the school building.
❷	操场在哪儿? Where is the sports field?	操场在体育馆(的)南边。 The sports field is to the south of the gymnasium.
❸	小伟在哪儿? Where is Xiaowei?	小伟在芳芳(的)旁边。 Xiaowei is beside Fangfang.

Note: The word 的 can be omitted for simplicity.

1. Refer to the school map shown on the left facing page and answer the following questions. There is more than one correct response to each question.

❶ 图书馆在哪儿?   ❹ 操场在哪儿?
❷ 体育馆在哪儿?   ❺ 教学楼在哪儿?
❸ 餐厅在哪儿?   ❻ 医务室在哪儿?

2. Work with a partner. You will take turns. Tell your partner who sits in front of, behind, to the left or to the right of you in class. Follow the example shown below:

小伟在我的前边，芳芳在我的后边。
安琪在我的左边，马克在我的右边。
我在大卫和玛丽的中间。

3. Answer the questions based on the dialog below. Then draw a map of the school as it was described in the conversation.

Student A:	Student B:
餐厅在哪儿?	餐厅在教学楼后边，医务室旁边。
电脑室呢?	电脑室在教学楼里。
教学楼大(dà, big)吗?	很大。教学楼里有很多(duō, many)教室。

❶ 餐厅在哪儿?
❷ 医务室在哪儿?
❸ 电脑室在哪儿?
❹ 教学楼在哪儿?
❺ 教学楼里有什么?

lí   yuǎn
你家离学校远吗?
Is your house far from the school?

① 我家离学校很远。
My house is far from the school.

28 miles

jìn
教室离图书馆近吗?
Is the classroom far from the libray?

② 教室离图书馆很近。
The classroom is quite near the libray.

图书馆

100 yards

教学楼

生 词

NEW WORDS

离 *prep.*	離	lí	*(in giving distances)* from
远 *adj.*	遠	yuǎn	far
近 *adj.*		jìn	near

LANGUAGE FOCUS

The preposition 离 means "from." It is used to form a prepositional structure indicating distance in space or time. The two commonly used structures are:

❶ A 离 B 很远 (A is far away from B)

❷ A 离 B 很近 (A is very close to B)

Examples:

Question

❶ 教室离图书馆远吗?
Is the classroom far from the library?

❷ 电脑室离医务室近吗?
Is the computer room near the medical room?

Answer

教室离图书馆很远。
The classroom is far from the library.

电脑室离医务室不近。
The computer room is not near the medical room?

1. Practice the following dialogs by replacing the underlined words with any two words in each of the boxes.

❶ Student A: 中国离美国远吗？
   Student B: 中国离美国很远。

英国　日本

❷ Student A: 你家离学校远吗？
   Student B: 我家离学校不远。

教室　图书馆

❸ Student A: 这儿离那儿近吗？
   Student B: 不近。

餐厅　操场

2. Find out how far your classmates live away from the school. Ask at least five of them the approximate distance between their house and the school, and fill in the table accordingly. If it is more than one mile, write 远 in the corresponding column. Write 近 if it is less.

Name	Distance	Far / Near
马克	2 miles	远

báibǎn
白板
white board

dìtú
地图
地　圖
map

zhōng
钟
鐘
clock

fěnbǐ
粉笔
粉　筆
chalk

shū
书
書
book

A Things in a classroom

生词 NEW WORDS

hēibǎn
黑板
blackboard

mén
门
門
door

chuānghu
窗户
窗　戶
window

qiáng
墙
wall

zhuōzi
桌子
desk

yǐzi
椅子
chair

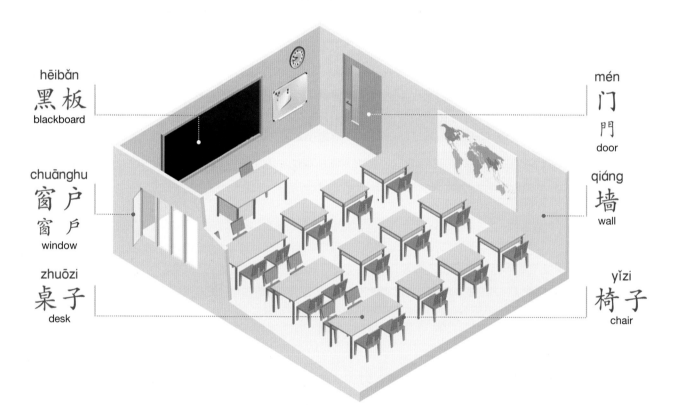

教室里有什么？
What's inside the classroom?

① 　zhuōzi　　 yǐzi　　 hēibǎn
　教室里有桌子、椅子和黑板。
There are chairs, tables and a blackboard.

墙上有什么？
What's on the wall?

báibǎn　zhōng
(2) 墙上有白板和钟。
On the wall are a white board and a clock.

❖ LANGUAGE FOCUS

上 can also be used as a directional word. When used after a noun, it forms a postpositional phrase that means "on or on the top of (noun)."

Examples: 桌子上, 墙上, 椅子上.

Now, you can ask and answer questions about what's on top of something.

Examples:

Question	Answer
❶ 墙上有什么？	墙上有地图。
What is on the wall?	There is a map on the wall.
❷ 桌子上有什么？	桌子上有书。
What is on the table?	There are two books on the table.

Try This!

Work with a classmate to describe what you see in these pictures. Use the following speech pattern as a guide:

Student A: 椅子上有什么？　　Student B: 椅子上有书。

You have learned the measure word 个 for time periods and people in Lessons 4 and 5 (e.g. 两个月, 三个星期; 一个哥哥, 三个男孩), and 只 and 条 for animals in lesson 6 (一只鸡, 三条鱼). Here is a list of other measure words for school items.

UNIT	M.W.		COLORS	PART.	OBJECTS	
一	个	the most common measure words for objects	hóngsè 红 色 紅 色 red	的	shūbāo 书 包 書 包 bag	
	個		lánsè 蓝 色 藍 色 blue	的	wénjùdài 文 具 袋 pencil case	
五	zhī 支	for long, thin, inflexible objects	huángsè 黄 色 黃 色 yellow	的	qiānbǐ 铅 笔 鉛 筆 pencil	
两 兩	枝		zǐsè 紫 色 purple	的	yuánzhūbǐ 圆 珠 笔 圓 珠 筆 pen	
一	zhāng 张 張	for paper products in pieces or sheets	báisè 白 色 white	的	zhǐ 纸 紙 paper	
一	bǎ 把	for tools with a handle or with something a person can hold	lǜsè 绿 色 綠 色 green	的	chǐzi 尺 子 ruler	
一	běn 本	for books of various kinds	hēisè 黑 色 black	的	shū 书 書 book	
一	kuài 块 塊	for something cubical or flat in shape	fěnhóngsè 粉 红 色 粉 紅 色 pink	的	xiàngpí 橡 皮 eraser	

Look around your classroom. What items do you see? What items do you carry in your backpack? Now, you can describe school items you and your classmates use every day. Here are some example sentences:

1. 我有一个红色的书包。
2. 小伟有两张白色的纸。
3. 她有三块蓝色的橡皮。
4. 桌子上有五本书。
5. 书包里有一个粉红色的文具袋和两本书。
6. 文具袋里有圆珠笔、铅笔、橡皮，还有一把尺子。

Try This!

1. Match the nouns with the correct measure words.

❶ 铅笔	张		❺ 橡皮	个
❷ 书包	本		❻ 圆珠笔	把
❸ 纸	个		❼ 文具袋	支
❹ 书	支		❽ 尺子	块

2. Describe the following pictures using the appropriate measure words and colors.

jiè   xíng
借我一支笔，行吗？
Could you lend me your pen, please?

gěi
行，给你。
Okay, here you go!

生词 NEW WORDS

借 v.	jiè	to lend; to borrow
行 v.	xíng	okay; will do
给 v. 給	gěi	give

LANGUAGE FOCUS

From time to time we all need to borrow things. In Chinese, we use the question structure "借 + (someone) + (something), 行吗？" when asking to borrow something.

Examples: 借我一把尺子，行吗？
Could you lend me your ruler?

The expressions 行吗？, 好吗？ and 可以吗？ all mean "Is it okay?" You may answer affirmatively using a simple 好! / 行! / 可以! or negatively with 不好! / 不行! / 不可以!

The verb 给 (to give) may be used in place of 借 to ask for something when you have no intention of returning it.

Examples: 爸爸给我一个电脑。
Dad gave me a computer.

Pretend you left your school bag at home and you need to borrow a pen, a pencil, a ruler, an eraser, and a notebook from your classmates. Your classmate may not be able to lend you an item if he/she has only one for him/herself. Continue to ask around until you have borrowed all five items. Use the following speech patterns for this activity:

Student A: 借我……，行吗？   Student B: 行，给你。

STEP 3
TALKING ABOUT COURSES AND CLASSES

kè
你有什么课？
What classes do you have (today)?

我有……课。
I have...

A Listing the courses one is taking

Zhōngwén
中文课
Chinese language class

Yīngyǔ
英语课
English language class

shùxué
数学课
mathematics class

diàn nǎo
电脑课
computer class

huàxué
化学课
chemistry class

měishù
美术课
art class

yīnyuè
音乐课
music class

shēngwù
生物课
biology class

wùlǐ
物理课
physics class

dìlǐ
地理课
geography class

lìshǐ
历史课
history class

tǐyù
体育课
physical education class

LANGUAGE FOCUS

The list above gives the most common subjects taught in schools. Now that you know how to say them in Chinese, you can talk about your favorite subjects at school, the classes you took last year, and what classes you will be taking this school year.

The word 课, which means "lesson/class/course," is added as a suffix to refer to a class or course for that subject.

Example: 数学课
math lesson

To ask what classes one is taking, you use the question phrase "有什么……？"

Example: 小伟有什么课？
What classes does Xiaowei have?

1. Draw lines to match the words on the left with the Chinese words on the right.

❶ History   中文   ❻ Mathematics   物理

❷ Biology   化学   ❼ Physics   地理

❸ English   生物   ❽ Art   音乐

❹ Chinese   历史   ❾ Geography   数学

❺ Chemistry   英语   ❿ Music   美术

2. Pretend you are engaged in the activities depicted in each picture. Work with your partner to ask and answer questions, following the speech pattern below:

Student A: 你有什么课？   Student B: 我有 <u>美术</u> 课。

CULTURAL HIGHLIGHTS

National College Entrance Exam

The National College Entrance Examination, commonly known as *Gao Kao*, is an academic examination held annually in mainland China. It is a prerequisite for entrance into almost all higher education institutions at the undergraduate level, and is usually taken by students in their last year of high school.

Chinese, mathematics, and a foreign language – usually English – are compulsory subjects in *Gao Kao*. For art students, there is a fourth subject test that integrates history, geography and political education. For science students, the fourth subject test integrates physics, chemistry and biology. Thus, the exam is called the "three plus X."

Students spend long hours studying in preparation for this examination, which is administered over a period of three days. Because this examination is essentially the only criterion for tertiary (university) education admission in China, poor performance on the exam often means that students will be denied a place in their desired course or college.

182

你有几门课?
How many classes do you have?

我有八门课。
I have eight classes.

LANGUAGE FOCUS

The measure word for courses is 门. Here is how you would ask and tell how many courses one is taking:

Examples:

❶ 你有几门课? 我有六门课。
How many classes do you have? I have six.

❷ 他有几门课? 他有七门课。
How many classes does he have? He has seven.

生 词

NEW WORDS

| 课 n. | 課 | kè | lesson; class; course |
| 门 m.w. | 門 | mén | (used for lesson / class / course) |

CULTURAL HIGHLIGHTS

Classroom System

In China, students in secondary schools are grouped together as a class and attend all lessons together. They take the same subjects and therefore share the same class schedule for the whole year. Each class usually stays in the same classroom and does not move between classrooms for different lessons. Instead, the teachers will go to the various classrooms to conduct their lessons.

Because of such a system, students in a class spend a lot of time together. They form strong bonds with each other and there is a strong sense of class spirit and cohesiveness. This togetherness reflects the Chinese culture of collectivism and unity.

In contrast to the Chinese classroom system, some schools around the world adopt a different system in which students move between classrooms for different lessons. One of the reasons is that students take different subjects and therefore have individual class schedules.

1. Read the dialog below and answer the following questions.

> 小伟： 马克，你有几门课？
>
> 马克： 中文、数学、英语、历史、地理、化学、
> 音乐、体育，我有八门课。你呢？
>
> 小伟： 我有六门课，中文、英语、数学、体育、音乐、历史。

❶ 马克有几门课？　　❷ 小伟有几门课？

2. Ask at least five of your classmates how many subjects they are taking and what they are. Record your findings in a table as shown below. Then determine who has the most number of classes and which subject is the most popular among the students. Use the following speech pattern for this activity:

> Student A: 你有几门课？
>
> Student B: 我有七门课，中文、数学、英语、历史、地理、化学和音乐。

Name	Number of subjects	Subjects taken
Annie	七门课	中文、数学、英语、历史、地理、化学、音乐

C Telling what courses one has taken

xué guo
你学过生物吗？
Have you taken a biology class?

我学过生物。
Yes, I have.

生 词

NEW WORDS

学 v.	學	xué	learn
过 part.	過	guo	(used after a verb to indicate the completion of an action)

你学过化学吗？
Have you taken a chemistry class?

我没学过化学。
No, I have not.

LANGUAGE FOCUS

Chinese verbs do not conjugate like the verbs of English. One way of expressing past tense is to use the aspect particle 过, which cannot stand by itself but can express completed actions when placed after verbs (e.g. 学过 means "have studied/learned"). The past negative is made by use of 没 or 没有, instead of 不.

1. Work with a classmate to practice the following speech pattern. Each will ask the other five questions and then switch roles.

Student A: 你学过……吗？   Student B: 我学过 / 没学过……。

2. Below is Mark's report card for the last school year. Study it and answer the following true-false questions.

Report Card

英语	中文	数学	物理	生物	地理
72	61	53	58	70	68

❶ Mark 学过中文和生物。 (　　)

❷ Mark 没学过化学和物理。 (　　)

❸ Mark 学过地理和历史。 (　　)

❹ Mark 没学过美术和音乐。 (　　)

STEP 1
DESCRIBING ONE'S SCHOOL

A teenager asking another about his or her school

你家离学校远吗？
　　我家离学校很远。
你们学校里有什么？
　　有教学楼，有体育馆，还有
　　图书馆。
有电脑室吗？
　　有。
在哪儿？
　　在教学楼后边。
电脑室离餐厅远吗？
　　不远。

STEP 2
DESCRIBING ONE'S CLASSROOM

A student bringing a friend to his/her classroom

你的教室在哪里？
　　在前边，离这里不远。
你教室里有什么？
　　有白板、桌子、椅子，还有
　　很多电脑。
你的桌子在哪里？
　　在那里，在窗户的右边。
你桌子上有什么？
　　有书，还有一个文具袋。
你的文具袋很大。里面有什么？
　　有铅笔、圆珠笔、橡皮，
　　还有一把绿色的尺子。

STEP 3
TALKING ABOUT COURSES AND CLASSES

A schoolmate asking another about his or her curriculum

你今天有什么课？
　　我有中文课、英语课、数学
　　课和历史课。
你最喜欢什么课？
　　我最喜欢中文课，也喜欢
　　数学课。
你今年学几门课？
　　八门。
很多啊！你学过生物吗？
　　我没学过生物，不过
　　明年我有生物课。

búguò
but

A classmate borrowing stationery from another

你有没有笔？
　　有。我有五支笔，都在我的
　　文具袋里。
你的文具袋在哪里？
　　在我的书包里。
你借我一支笔，行吗？
　　行，给你。
谢谢！

Step Up!

1. Read Mark's description of his school. Draw a map based on the description and use it to answer the following questions.

我的学校不大也不小。教学楼里有四个教室。最右边是绿色的教室，它的旁边是白色的教室。最左边是蓝色的教室。在蓝色和白色的教室中间是黄色的教室。

教学楼外有一个图书馆，有一个体育馆，还有一个餐厅。体育馆在图书馆的前边，餐厅在图书馆的后边。我最喜欢体育馆。

❶ 马克的学校大不大？

❷ 绿色的教室在哪儿？

❸ 蓝色的教室在哪儿？

❹ 图书馆在哪儿？

❺ 体育馆在哪儿？

❻ 教学楼里有什么？

❼ 白色的教室在哪儿？

❽ 黄色的教室在哪儿？

❾ 他最喜欢什么地方？

2. CONNECTIONS: MATHEMATICS AND STATISTICS

Find out the number of students in your class taking various subjects, such as English, Chinese, mathematics, history, geography, Iterature, physics, art, etc. Ask all of the questions in Chinese. Use the information to plot a graph to see which subjects are the most or least popular among the students. Compare your findings with your classmates.

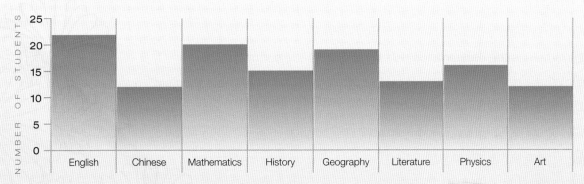

3. Write a short introduction of your school in Chinese. Include information such as the school's location, its facilities, the number of students enrolled, the number of staff, and the types of courses offered. Put your school introduction in your portfolio. *Example:*

我们的学校很大。
学校里有教学楼、一个图书馆……

Fun Time!

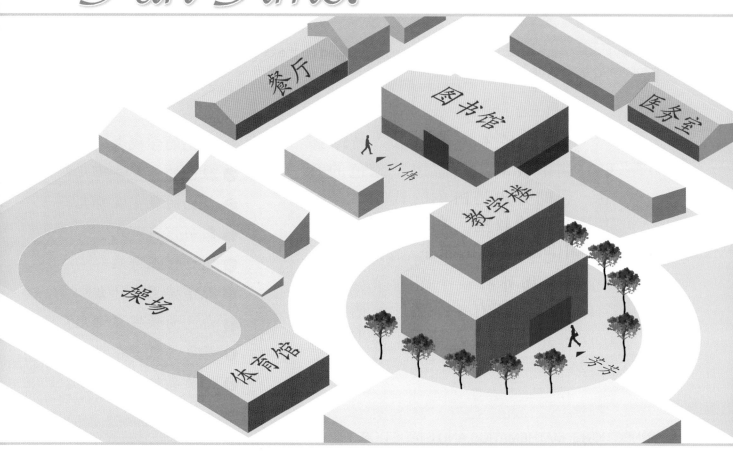

You have learned to specify locations using position words (前边, 后边, 左边, 右边, 旁边, 中间). In this activity, you will apply what you have learned to answer the following questions in Chinese based on the school map above.

❶ What are the facilities found in this school?

❷ Where is the cafeteria located in relation to the school building?

❸ Where is the sports field located? What other facility is near the field?

❹ Where is the library located?

❺ Where is Fangfang? And Xiaowei?

❻ Where is the infirmary located?

❼ Is the library far from the school building?

❽ Is the gymnasium far from the medical room?

❾ On a piece of paper, write out the position words and place them in the correct positions based on their meanings.

I have learned...

Core Vocabulary

学校 n.	學校	xuéxiào	school	门 n.	門	mén	door
教室 n.		jiàoshì	classroom	地图 n.	地圖	dìtú	map
图书馆 n.	圖書館	túshūguǎn	library	钟 n.	鐘	zhōng	clock
餐厅 n.		cāntīng	cafeteria	粉笔 n.	粉筆	fěnbǐ	chalk
教学楼 n.	教學樓	jiàoxuélóu	school building (where classes are held)	书 n.	書	shū	book
体育馆 n.	體育館	tǐyùguǎn	gymnasium	书包 n.	書包	shūbāo	bag
操场 n.	操場	cāochǎng	sports field	文具袋 n.		wénjùdài	pencil case
电脑室 n.	電腦室	diànnǎoshì	computer room	橡皮 n.		xiàngpí	eraser
医务室 n.	醫務室	yīwùshì	medical room	铅笔 n.	鉛筆	qiānbǐ	pencil
里(边) n.	裏(邊)	lǐ(bian)	inside	圆珠笔 n.	圓珠筆	yuánzhūbǐ	pen
外(边) n.	外(邊)	wài(bian)	outside	纸 n.	紙	zhǐ	paper
前边 n.	前邊	qiánbian	in the front	尺子 n.		chǐzi	ruler
后边 n.	後邊	hòubian	behind	本 m.w.		běn	(used for books of various kinds)
左边 n.	左邊	zuǒbian	on the left	支 m.w.	枝	zhī	(used for long, thin and inflexible objects)
右边 n.	右邊	yòubian	on the right	块 m.w.	塊	kuài	(used for something cubical or flat in shape)
旁边 n.	旁邊	pángbiān	beside	把 m.w.		bǎ	(for tools with a handle or with something a person can hold)
中间 n.	中間	zhōngjiān	in the middle	张 m.w.	張	zhāng	(used for paper products in pieces or sheets)
离 prep.	離	lí	(in giving distances) from	借 v.		jiè	to lend; to borrow
远 adj.	遠	yuǎn	far	行 v.		xíng	okay; will do
近 adj.		jìn	near	给 v.	給	gěi	give
桌子 n.		zhuōzi	desk	英语 n.	英語	Yīngyǔ	English language
椅子 n.		yǐzi	chair	中文 n.		Zhōngwén	Chinese language
窗户 n.	窗戶	chuānghu	window	课 n.	課	kè	lesson; class; course
黑板 n.		hēibǎn	blackboard	门 m.w.	門	mén	(used for lesson/class/course)
白板 n.		báibǎn	white board	学 v.	學	xué	learn; study
墙 n.		qiáng	wall	过 part.	過	guo	(used after a verb to indicate the completion of an action)

Extended Vocabulary

红色 n.	红色	hóngsè	red		电脑 n.		diànnǎo	computer
蓝色 n.	藍色	lánsè	blue		历史 n.	歷史	lìshǐ	history
黄色 n.	黃色	huángsè	yellow		物理 n.		wùlǐ	physics
绿色 n.	綠色	lǜsè	green		化学 n.	化學	huàxué	chemistry
白色 n.		báisè	white		地理 n.		dìlǐ	geography
紫色 n.		zǐsè	purple		生物 n.		shēngwù	biology
黑色 n.		hēisè	black		体育 n.	體育	tǐyù	physical education
粉红色 n.	粉紅色	fěnhóngsè	pink		美术 n.	美術	měishù	art
数学 n.	數學	shùxué	mathematics		音乐 n.	音樂	yīnyuè	music

 SENTENCE PATTERNS

学校里有什么？学校里有教学楼，有图书馆，还有体育馆。

教学楼外有什么？教学楼外有操场。

你家离学校远吗？我家离学校很远。

教室离图书馆近吗？教室离图书馆很近。

教室里有什么？教室里有黑板、桌子和椅子。

墙上有什么？墙上有白板和钟。

借我一支笔，行吗？行，给你。

你有什么课？

你有几门课？我有八门课。

你学过生物吗？我学过生物。你学过化学吗？我没学过化学。

I can do!

Interpretive Communication

❑ I can understand when someone talks about the facilities in his/her school.

❑ I can understand when someone describes common classroom items and their locations.

❑ I can understand when someone states the color of an object.

❑ I can understand when someone talks about his/her school schedule.

Interpersonal Communication

❑ I can exchange information about the facilities in a school.

❑ I can ask for and give directions.

❑ I can ask and answer questions about classroom items.

❑ I can exchange information about courses offered at my school.

Presentational Communication

❑ I can use a map and tell the whereabouts of different buildings in my school.

❑ I can give a short introduction of my school.

❑ I can describe the things I see in my classroom.

❑ I can talk about the courses I am taking and my favorite subject.

Cultural Knowledge

❑ I can talk about the similarities and differences between educational systems in China and the United States.

❑ I can explain the differences between classroom systems in China and the United States.

❑ I can talk about the requirements of China's National College Entrance Exam.

My busy schedule

天天都很忙

COMMUNICATIVE GOALS

- Talking about one's class schedule
- Describing one's daily routine
- Talking about after-school activities
- Expressing where and when one does an activity

CULTURAL KNOWLEDGE

- Class schedule of a typical Chinese middle school
- English language learning in China
- Extracurricular activities offered in schools in China
- Daily morning and eye exercises practiced in schools in China

Get ready...

Below is a typical middle school's class schedule in China. Study it and answer the following questions:

- What subjects are taught at this school?
- Do you study the same subjects?
- Which subjects have the most number of class periods per week? Why do you think this is so?
- How many classes do these students have in a day?
- What is the school dismissal time? Do you think it is early or late?
- Give at least two similarities and two differences between this class schedule and yours.

课程表 (kèchéngbiǎo, class schedule)

	星期一	星期二	星期三	星期四	星期五
8.00 – 8.45	英语	数学	化学	物理	英语
9.00 – 9.45	中文	物理	中文	数学	中文
10.00 – 10.30	课间操 (kèjiāncāo, morning exercise)				
10.30 – 11.15	数学	历史	数学	英语	数学
11.30 – 12.15	物理	英语	英语	中文	历史
12.30 – 2.00	午休 (wǔxiū, noon break)				
2.00 – 2.45	地理	美术	地理	音乐	化学
3.00 – 3.45	化学	中文	体育	美术	体育
7.00 – 9.00	晚自习 (wǎnzìxí, night study)				

今天很忙!

STEPS *at a glance!*

STEP 1

ABOUT ONE'S CLASS SCHEDULE

A. Asking what class one has on a certain day

你今天有什么课?

我今天有英语课。

B. Number of class periods

你今天有几节课?

我今天有六节课。

C. Class starting and ending times

你今天几点上课? 几点下课?

STEP 2

MORE ABOUT ONE'S CLASS SCHEDULE

A. Asking what class one has before/ after a certain time

十点以前是什么课?

十点以后是什么课?

B. Asking what class one has at a specific time period

明天从九点到十点你有什么课?

我有中文课。

STEP 3

ABOUT ONE'S DAILY SCHEDULE

A. Daily routines

你几点起床?

我早上七点半起床。

B. Expressing where and when one does an activity

你在哪儿上课?

我在教室上课。

C. Talking about what one did after school

昨天晚上你做什么了?

我上网了。

193

你今天有什么课？
What classes do you have today?

(1) 我今天有英语课。
I have English class today.

星期一你有什么课？
What classes do you have on Monday?

(2) 星期一我有中文课。
I have Chinese class on Monday.

LANGUAGE FOCUS

To ask about the classes one has on a particular day or at a certain time, place the time word before the verb 有.

Examples:

Question	Answer
❶ 你上午有什么课？ What classes do you have in the morning?	我上午有数学课。 I have math class in the morning.
❷ 她星期三有什么课？ What classes does she have on Wednesday?	她星期三有英语课。 She has English class on Wednesday.

The other way to say the same thing is to place the time word before the subject.

Examples:

Question	Answer
❶ 上午你有什么课？	上午我有数学课。
❷ 星期三她有什么课？	星期三她有英语课。

1. Use the words below to form sentences.

❶ 我　　　　数学　　星期三　⟶　我星期三有数学课。
❷ 小丽　　　历史　　今天
❸ 安琪　　　法语　　星期二和星期五
❹ 他哥哥　　美术　　后天
❺ 小伟　　　地理　　星期一和星期四
❻ 她妹妹　　化学　　下午
❼ 我姐姐　　电脑　　星期三、星期四和星期五

2. Work with a classmate to find out his/her weekly schedule. Record your findings in the chart below. Refer to the speech pattern to ask and answer the questions:

Student A: 你……有什么课？　　　Student B: 我……有……课。

Weekly Schedule

Day / Time	星期一	星期二	星期三	星期四	星期五

CULTURAL HIGHLIGHTS

English Language Learning Frenzy

In China, English is widely regarded as an important language to acquire for success in an increasingly globalized world. It is a compulsory subject in school, and students usually attend six periods of English class in a typical week. Besides learning the subject in school, many students spend extra hours outside class time taking enrichment or tuition classes offered by private language schools. Parents make every effort to sign their children up for such courses, and are often willing to send them for expensive learning trips to English speaking countries during vacation so that they can improve their English language skills by immersing themselves in an English-speaking environment.

Lots of English dictionaries in bookstores in China

In order to host the Olympics in Beijing in 2008, a massive English-learning campaign was launched to encourage citizens to learn and use English. The campaign was a huge success and many people improved their English language skills.

Does your country exhibit the same frenzy for learning a particular language? Share it with the class and explain why there is such a frenzy.

B Number of class periods

jié
你今天有几节课？
How many class periods do you have today?

我今天有六节课。
I have six class periods today.

NEW WORDS 生 词

| 课 n. | 课 | kè | class period |
| 节 m.w. | 節 | jié | (used for class periods) |

LANGUAGE FOCUS

The measure word for class periods is 节.

Examples:

1 三节课 three class periods
2 五节课 five class periods
3 两节数学课 two class periods of math

When 节 is placed after an ordinal number, it refers to that class period of the day.

Examples:

1 第六节课 The 6th class period
2 第八节课 The 8th class period

Study the class schedule below and answer the following questions in Chinese.

Class Schedule

	星期一	星期二	星期三	星期四	星期五
一	英语	中文	中文	英语	中文
二	中文	英语	英语	中文	英语
三	数学	历史	地理	物理	数学
四	美术	数学	数学	化学	历史
五	化学	物理	美术	数学	体育
六	体育	生物	体育	生物	地理

1 星期一有几节课？
2 一个星期有几节英语课？
3 星期几有音乐课？
4 有几门课？

生 词

NEW WORDS

上课 phr.	上課	shàngkè	to attend class; class starts
下课 phr.	下課	xiàkè	to finish class; class ends
上学 phr.	上學	shàngxué	to attend school
放学 phr.	放學	fàngxué	to leave school upon dismissal

shàngkè   xiàkè

你今天几点上课？几点下课？
What time does your class start today? What time does it end?

1   我今天上午八点上课，九点下课。
My class starts at eight in the morning, and ends at nine.

shàngxué   fàngxué

你今天几点上学？几点放学？
What time do you go to school today? What time do you leave school?

2   我今天上午八点上学，下午三点放学。
I go to school at eight in the morning and leave at three in the afternoon.

LANGUAGE FOCUS

When placed after a time expression, 上课 / 下课 and 上学 / 放学 are used to state the start/end time of a class period and a school day, respectively.

Examples:

❶ 我八点上课，十点下课。
My class starts at eight o'clock, and ends at ten.

❷ 我七点上学，五点放学。
I go to school at seven o'clock and leave school at five.

1. Arrange the words below to form sentences.

   ❶ 我　　　上课　九点　　明天 ——→ 我明天九点上课。
   ❷ 上学　　她　　八点　　每天
   ❸ 今天　　你　　下课　　几点
   ❹ 他　　　放学　星期三　五点
   ❺ 星期五　下课　三点　　我

2. Ask five of your classmates what time they arrived and left school yesterday. Record your findings in the chart below. Refer to the following speech pattern when asking and answering questions.

   Student A:
   你昨天几点上学？

   Student B:
   我昨天……上学。

Name of student / Time	Start Time	End Time
David	9 am	3 pm

 CULTURAL HIGHLIGHTS

Extra-curricular Activities

In China, there are a wide range of extra-curricular activities for students to choose from. These activities are usually organized and run by teachers and students, and can be conducted inside or outside the school campus. Instructors or coaches are engaged to provide specialized training in certain fields.

Extra-curricular activities that are unique to schools in China include *Wushu* (Chinese martial arts), Chinese orchestra, table-tennis and badminton. These sports are very popular among students and most schools offer them as extra-curricular activities. Such popularity creates a massive talent pool from which the best players are selected for the national team. In a way, this explains why China excels in these sports.

Schools around the world have their own areas of popular extra-curricular activities. What are the popular ones in your school? What new activities would you like your school to have?

生词 NEW WORDS

现在
now

现在十点。

英语课

yǐqián
以前
before

yǐhòu
以后
以後
after

数学课

A Asking what class one has before/after a certain time

yǐqián
十点以前是什么课？
What is the class before 10 o'clock?

① 十点以前是英语课。
The class before 10 o'clock is English.

yǐhòu
十点以后是什么课？
What is the class after 10 o'clock?

② 十点以后是数学课。
The class after 10 o'clock is math.

LANGUAGE FOCUS

以前 is used for something that occurs before a certain time. 以后 is used for something that occurs after a certain time. Unlike the English prepositions "before" and "after" which are placed before a time expression (e.g. before 5pm), 以前 and 以后 are placed after a time expression (e.g. 五点以前).

For example:
❶ 十点以前是什么课？
  十点以前是英语课。

❷ 历史课以后是什么课？
  历史课以后是地理课。

In English, the prepositions "before" and "after" are usually placed before the time or event. In Chinese, as mentioned earlier, they are placed after.

For example: ❶ 下午三点以前是历史课。 Before 3 pm is history class.

❷ 中文课以后是英语课。 After Chinese class is English class.

1. Work with a classmate to ask and answer the following questions.

   ❶ 这节课以前是什么课？

   ❷ 你明天八点以后有没有课？

   ❸ 你十二点以后有什么课？

   ❹ 你今天下午两点以前有什么课？

   ❺ 今天下午三点以后你有课吗？

2. **Pair Work:** Each pair will receive two incomplete schedules. Each schedule contains information that the other schedule is lacking. Take one of the schedules and ask your partner with the other schedule some questions so that you can complete each other's schedule.

   Example: Student A: 星期一数学课以后是什么课？

                   Student B: 星期一数学课以后是电脑课。

 CULTURAL HIGHLIGHTS

Morning Exercise

Every day students in elementary, middle, and high schools in China do a form of morning exercise called 课间操 (kèjiāncāo). Between the second and third periods, all students walk down to the sports field to do these exercises for 20 minutes. As students do the exercises, music is generally played over the loud speaker to help students do the exercises in sync with one another. These exercises consist of stretching, bending, jumping jacks, and other warm-up movements. Such exercises may help students relax and also improve their general health.

cóng   dào
明天从九点到十点你有什么课？
What class do you have tomorrow from 9 to 10?

我有中文课。
I have Chinese class.

NEW WORD

| 从…到… | 從…到… | cóng...dào | from...to... |

LANGUAGE FOCUS

"从…到…" can be used to refer to a specific time period. It literally means "from one point of time to the other." Place the starting time after 从 and the ending time after 到 to form a time period. The pattern for this is 从 + starting time + 到 + ending time.

Example: ❶ 从九点到十点你有什么课？我有数学课。

❷ 从早上到下午你有什么课？
我有中文课、英语课、化学课和历史课。

You can also add other time words at the beginning to indicate time periods on other days.

Examples: ❶ 星期一从八点到九点你有什么课？我有中文课。

❷ 明天从两点到三点你有什么课？我有英语课。

❸ 星期三从十点到十一点有数学课。

1. Complete the class schedule using information provided by the sentences below.

   ❶ 星期一从九点到十点有中文课。

   ❷ 星期三从下午一点到两点有美术课。

   ❸ 星期五从八点到九点有英语课。

   ❹ 星期二从十一点到十二点有数学课。

   ❺ 星期四从下午两点到三点有体育课。

   ❻ 星期一从十点到十一点有数学课。

   ❼ 星期四从八点到九点有中文课。

   ❽ 星期二从十点到十一点有物理课。

   ❾ 星期五从下午两点到三点有化学课。

   ❿ 星期三从九点到十点有中文课。

   ⓫ 星期五从十一点到十二点有地理课。

   ⓬ 星期三从下午两点到三点有地理课。

Time Schedule

	星期一	星期二	星期三	星期四	星期五
8:00 – 9:00	英语	中文	英语		
9:00 – 10:00		英语		英语	中文
10:00 – 11:00			数学	物理	数学
11:00 – 12:00	化学		化学	数学	
12:00 – 1:00	Lunch Break				
1:00 – 2:00	历史	音乐		历史	音乐
2:00 – 3:00	体育	美术			

2. Using the completed class schedule above, work with a classmate to ask and answer at least five questions based on the schedule. You can refer to the speech pattern below.

Student A:	Student B:
星期＿＿＿从＿＿＿到＿＿＿有什么课？	有＿＿＿上课。

A Daily routines

07:30

qǐchuáng
起床 *phr.*
to get out of bed

qǐchuáng
你几点起床？
What time do you wake up?

我早上七点半起床。
I wake up at 7.30 am.

生 词 NEW WORDS

07:40

xǐliǎn
洗脸 *phr.*
洗 臉
to wash one's face

08:15

chī zǎofàn
吃早饭 *phr.*
吃 早 飯
to eat breakfast

16:00

zuò gōngkè
做功课 *phr.*
做 功 课
to do homework

07:45

shuāyá
刷牙 *phr.*
to brush one's teeth

08:45

shàngxué
上学 *phr.*
上 學
to go to school

19:00

chī wǎnfàn
吃晚饭 *phr.*
吃 晚 飯
to eat dinner

07:50

xǐzǎo
洗澡 *phr.*
to bathe;
to take a shower

12:00

chī wǔfàn
吃午饭 *phr.*
吃 午 飯
to eat lunch

20:00

kàn diànshì
看电视 *phr.*
看 電 視
to watch TV

08:00

chuān yīfu
穿衣服 *phr.*
to get dressed;
put on clothes

15:00

fàngxué
放学 *phr.*
放 學
to leave school
(upon dismissal)

22:00

shuìjiào
睡觉 *phr.*
睡 覺
to go to bed; to sleep

The same sentence pattern you used to ask someone the time he/she attends class (你今天几点上课?) may be used to ask for the time when other activities are carried out. Simply replace 上课 with the activity in question. To reply, retain the word order and replace 几点 with the time expression.

Examples:

❶ 你们几点吃午饭? 我们中午十二点吃午饭。
What time do you eat lunch? We have lunch at noon.

❷ 她几点睡觉? 她晚上十一点睡觉。
What time does she go to bed? She goes to bed at 11 pm.

Try This!

1. Put the following activities in a logical order.

吃早饭	放学	洗脸	上学
睡觉	吃午饭	吃晚饭	看电视
做功课	起床	刷牙	洗澡

2. Go around the class and ask five of your classmates what time they carry out their daily routine, and then write down their responses. Follow the speech pattern below:

Student A: 你几点吃早饭?   Student B: 我八点吃早饭。

同学的名字	吃早饭	吃午饭	吃晚饭	睡觉
大卫	8 am	1 pm	7.30 pm	11 pm

2. State the activity shown in each picture and the time it was performed. Follow the example given.

大卫早上**7**点起床。

爸爸＿＿＿＿＿＿＿＿＿＿＿＿＿＿＿＿＿＿＿＿。

安琪＿＿＿＿＿＿＿＿＿＿＿＿＿＿＿＿＿＿。

玛丽＿＿＿＿＿＿＿＿＿＿＿＿＿＿＿＿＿＿。

弟弟＿＿＿＿＿＿＿＿＿＿＿＿＿＿＿＿＿＿。

姐姐＿＿＿＿＿＿＿＿＿＿＿＿＿＿＿＿＿＿。

你在哪儿上课？
Where do you have your class?

我在教室上课。
I have my class in the classroom.

生 词 NEW WORDS

yùshì
浴室 n.
bathroom

cāntīng
餐厅 n.
餐廳
dining room

shūfáng
书房 n.
書房
study room

kètīng
客厅 n.
客廳
living room

wòshì
卧室 n.
bedroom

LANGUAGE FOCUS

"在 + 哪儿" forms a question phrase meaning "where." To ask where someone does an activity, place the question phrase 在哪儿 before the action. When replying, retain the word order and replace 在哪儿 with the location word.

Examples: ❶ 你在哪儿看电视？我在客厅看电视。
Where do you watch TV? I watch TV in the living room.

❷ 他在哪儿做功课？他在书房做功课。
Where does he do his homework? He does his homework in the study room.

While stating the location where an activity takes place, you can also add the time expression before the action. Think of creating the sentence this way: person (who), time expression (when), location word (where), and activity (action).

Examples: ❶ 我九点在教室上课。
I have my lesson at 9 am in the classroom.

❷ 他晚上八点在客厅看电视。
He watches TV at 8 pm in the living room.

Try This!

1. Look at each picture, and decide if the caption beside it accurately describes the picture or not.

T / F

玛丽在浴室洗脸。

T / F

叔叔在卧室睡觉。

T / F

姐姐在图书馆看书。

T / F

小伟在动物园看熊猫。

T / F

马克在客厅看电视。

T / F

安琪在教室吃午饭。

T / F

哥哥在电脑室做功课。

T / F

芳芳在教室上课。

2. Work with a classmate to ask and answer questions on the following activities. Use the word bank below to choose one place where it would be appropriate to do the activity in question.

电脑室	操场	浴室	教室	客厅	图书馆
体育馆	卧室	书房	餐厅	食堂	学校

For example:

Student A: 你在哪儿吃早饭？   Student B: 我在餐厅吃早饭。

❶ 吃早饭   ❻ 看电视

❷ 做功课   ❼ 洗脸

❸ 吃午饭   ❽ 睡觉

❹ 上课   ❾ 刷牙

❺ 吃晚饭   ❿ 洗澡

le

昨天晚上你做什么了？

What did you do last night?

shàngwǎng

我上网了。

I went on the Internet.

 生 词 NEW WORDS

dǎ diànhuà
打电话 *phr.*
打電話
to make a phone call

fā duǎnxìn
发短信 *phr.*
發短信
to send text messages

shàngwǎng
上网 *phr.*
上網
to go on the Internet

fā diànyóu
发电邮 *phr.*
發電郵
to send e-mails

(shàngwǎng) liáotiān
（上网）聊天 *phr.*

to chat online

xiě bókè
写博客 *phr.*
寫博客
to write a blog

wán diànnǎo yóuxì
玩电脑游戏 *phr.*
玩電腦遊戲
to play computer games

dǎ diàndòng
打电动 *phr.*
打電動
to play console games

kàn diànyǐng
看电影 *phr.*
看電影
to watch a movie

dǎqiú
打球 *phr.*

to play ball

LANGUAGE FOCUS

The particle 了 is placed at the end of the sentence to indicate that something has taken place.

Examples: ❶ 昨天晚上你做什么了？我打电动了。
What did you do last night? I played electronic games.

❷ 昨天下午你做什么了？我看电影了。
What did you do this afternoon? I watched a movie.

To show that an action has never occurred, add 没 or 没有 before the verb and omit 了.

Example: ❶ 昨天晚上你上网了吗？我没上网，我做功课了。
Did you go on the Internet last night? No, I didn't. I did my homework.

1. Rewrite the following sentences to show that each activity has taken place. You may include the time and location where it took place.

❶ 我吃午饭。 ⟶ 我吃午饭了。
⟶ 我十二点在餐厅吃午饭了。

❷ 他发电邮。
❸ 她洗澡。
❹ 我做功课。
❺ 哥哥上网。
❻ 姐姐发短信。

❼ 马克打球。
❽ 芳芳看电影。
❾ 妹妹上网聊天。
❿ 弟弟玩电脑游戏。

2. Ask at least six classmates to find out five main activities they did after school yesterday, and then record their responses to determine the most popular after-school activity among students in your class. Conduct the survey using the speech pattern below:

Student A: 你昨天做什么了？

Student B: 我昨天上网了，做功课了，看电视了，发短信了，还玩电脑游戏了。

同学的名字	Activity 1	Activity 2	Activity 3	Activity 4	Activity 5
小伟	上网	做功课	看电视	发短信	玩电脑游戏

STEP 1
ABOUT ONE'S CLASS SCHEDULE

Two students exchanging information about their class schedules

明天上午你有什么课？
　　我有中文课、数学课和
　　物理课。
你一个星期有几节中文课？
　　有两节，星期二和星期四。
我有一节中文课，在星期三。
　　你明天几点放学？
下午两点。你呢？
　　我下午三点下课。

STEP 3
ABOUT ONE'S DAILY SCHEDULE

Two students talking about what they did last Saturday

你星期六晚上做什么了？
　　我看电影了。你呢？
我在家上网了，还写博客了。
　　玩电脑游戏了吗？
没有。下个星期六下午我们去打
球，好吗？
　　好！

STEP 2
MORE ABOUT ONE'S CLASS SCHEDULE

One student asking another about what class he/she has at a specific time period

今天下午从两点到三点你有
什么课？
　　我有体育课。你呢？
我有美术课。三点以后你有
课吗？
　　没有。你呢？
我也没有课。
　　我们去图书馆，好吗？
好。

One student asking another about what class he/she has before and after a certain time

十点以前是什么课？
　　十点以前是英语课。
十点以后呢？
　　十点以后是中文课。
今天有数学课吗？
　　今天没有数学课，下午有
　　一节生物课。

Step Up!

1. Draw up your class schedule in Chinese and present it to the class. Talk about the subjects you are taking, the number of class periods you have each day, and the class starting and ending times. Allow your classmates to ask questions.

2. Imagine you are attending a school in China. Make up a new class schedule for yourself. Decide what subjects you would like to take, but make sure that your subject combinations meet the requirements of China's National College Entrance Examination. Then, write at least five sentences about your schedule. When you are done, save a copy of the schedule in your portfolio.

Examples:

我星期一上中文课、英语课和数学课。
星期二上……。

我早上七点上学，下午五点放学。

3. Below is a blog entry by a Chinese student about her day at school. Read it and write a similar blog entry describing your day at school.

	Share Next Blogs >>		Create Blog Sign in

Wednesday, May 12, 2012

今天我早上七点半上学，七点三刻上课。

上午有四节课：中文、数学、历史、英语。

中间有课间操，学生在操场做体操 (tǐcāo, exercise)。

中午有四十五分钟午休。

下午还有两节课：美术、地理。

下午四点放学。

回家 (huíjiā, return home) 以后，我在书房做功课、
上网聊天。

晚饭以后，我在客厅看电视。

洗澡以后，我晚上十点睡觉。

今天我很忙！

Fun Time!

Ocular exercise 眼保健操
<small>bǎo jiàn</small>

Elementary and middle school students in China are required to do eye exercises twice a day. This is a longstanding practice which dates back to the early 1970s. The aim is to reduce the rate of eye disorders among students.

Accompanying music is played while students do the eye exercises. Students will follow the instructions and massage the various acupuncture points around the eyes according to the rhythm of the music.

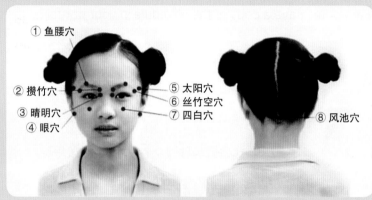

Various acupuncture points around the eyes

yúyāo xuè	① 鱼腰穴	
cuánzhú	② 攒竹穴	
qíngmíng	③ 晴明穴	
	④ 眼穴	
tàiyáng	⑤ 太阳穴	
sīzhúkōng	⑥ 丝竹空穴	
sìbái	⑦ 四白穴	
fēngchí	⑧ 风池穴	

The eye exercises consist of six segments:

1. Massage the Cuanzhu point ② using the thumbs.

2. Massage the Qingming point ③ using the forefingers.

3. Massage the Sibai point ⑦ using the forefingers.

4. Massage the temples ⑤ and the eyebrow area ① ⑥ using the thumbs and the sides of the forefingers.

5. Massage the Fengchi points ⑧ using the forefingers and middle fingers.

6. Massage the Yan point ④ at the earlobe using the thumb and forefinger.

I have learned...

Core Vocabulary

课 n.	课	kè	class period		吃午饭 phr.	吃午饭	chī wǔfàn	to eat lunch
节 m.w.	節	jié	(used for class periods)		吃晚饭 phr.	吃晚飯	chī wǎnfàn	to eat dinner
上学 phr.	上學	shàngxué	to attend school		做功课 phr.	做功課	zuò gōngkè	to do homework
上课 phr.	上课	shàngkè	to attend class; class starts		穿衣服 phr.		chuān yīfu	to get dressed; put on clothes
放学 phr.	放學	fàngxué	to leave school (upon dismissal)		睡觉 phr.	睡覺	shuìjiào	to go to bed; to sleep
下课 phr.	下課	xiàkè	to finish class; class ends		看电影 phr.	看電影	kàn diànyǐng	to watch a movie
以前 n.		yǐqián	before		看电视 phr.	看電視	kàn diànshì	to watch TV
以后 n.	以後	yǐhòu	after		浴室 n.		yùshì	bathroom
从…到…	從…到…	cóng dào	from…to…		卧室 n.	臥室	wòshì	bedroom
起床 phr.		qǐchuáng	to get out of bed		餐厅 n.	餐廳	cāntīng	dining room
洗脸 phr.	洗臉	xǐliǎn	to wash one's face		客厅 n.	客廳	kètīng	living room
刷牙 phr.		shuāyá	to brush one's teeth		书房 n.	書房	shūfáng	study room
洗澡 phr.		xǐzǎo	to bathe; to take a shower		了 part.		le	(used at the end of a sentence to indicate that something has taken place)
吃早饭 phr.	吃早飯	chī zǎofàn	to eat breakfast					

Extended Vocabulary

发电邮 phr.	發電郵	fā diànyóu	to send e-mails
玩电脑游戏 phr.	玩電腦游戲	wán diànnǎo yóuxì	to play computer games
发短信 phr.	發短信	fā duǎnxìn	to send text messages
打电动 phr.	打電動	dǎ diàndòng	to play console games
上网 phr.	上網	shàngwǎng	to go on the Internet
打球 phr.		dǎqiú	to play ball
打电话 phr.	打電話	dǎ diànhuà	to make a phone call
写博客 phr.	寫博客	xiě bókè	to write a blog
(上网)聊天 phr.	(上網)聊天	(shàngwǎng)liáotiān	to chat online

你今天有什么课？我今天有英语课。

星期一你有什么课？星期一我有中文课。

你今天有几节课？我今天有六节课。

你今天几点上课？几点下课？我今天早上八点上课，九点下课。

你今天几点上学？几点放学？我今天上午八点上学，下午三点放学。

现在十点。

十点以前是什么课？十点以前是英语课。

十点以后是什么课？十点以后是数学课。

明天从九点到十点你有什么课？我有中文课。

你几点起床？我早上七点半起床。

你在哪儿上课？我在教室上课。

昨天晚上你做什么了？我上网了。

I can do!

Interpretive **Communication**

❑ I can understand when my classmates tell me about their typical day at school.

❑ I can understand when someone describes his or her daily routine.

❑ I can understand when someone recalls the activities he or she did after school.

Interpersonal **Communication**

❑ I can exchange information about class schedules with my classmates and others.

❑ I can ask and answer questions about one's daily routine, giving details of time and place.

❑ I can exchange information about after-school activities.

❑ I can invite a friend to spend time together.

Presentational **Communication**

❑ I can give detailed information about my weekly class schedule.

❑ I can describe my daily routine.

❑ I can talk about what I do in my free time.

Cultural **Knowledge**

❑ I can tell the differences between a middle school class schedule in China and the United States.

❑ I can share information about daily exercises practiced en masse in schools in China.

❑ I can talk about how Chinese students are learning the English language.

❑ I can state some of the most popular school extracurricular activities in China.

❑ I can do some simple eye exercises.

LESSON 9

My interests, my dreams

我的爱好

COMMUNICATIVE GOALS
- Talking about one's interests and hobbies
- Talking about one's abilities and skills
- Stating one's dream job
- Exchanging information about time spent on hobbies

Cultural Knowledge
- Ping pong diplomacy
- The Four Arts of a Chinese scholar
- The origin and key characteristics of Taiji

Get ready...

Below is a blog entry by a teenager about a movie he saw. New words have been marked with pinyin and English translations. Read the entry and answer the questions that follow.

二〇〇九年十二月二十日，星期五

| Share | Next Blogs >> | | Create Blog | Sign in |

星期天下午三点，我和
朋友去看电影《阿凡达》了。
péngyou kàn fándá
friend watch Avatar

电影很好看。

我最喜欢电影里那条龙，
它很大，还会飞。

看了《阿凡达》，我想学习动画制作，
xiǎng xí dònghuà zhìzuò
want learn animation making

以后当电影制作人。
dāng
be producer

1. Does the teenager like the movie?
2. What features in the movie interest him?
3. How does this interest impact him?

我将来想当什么？

STEP 1

ABOUT ONE'S INTERESTS AND HOBBIES

A. Sports and games

你有什么爱好？我喜欢游泳。

B. The arts and music

你的爱好是什么？

我的爱好是唱歌。

STEP 2

ABOUT ONE'S ABILITIES AND SKILLS

A. Asking about one's ability to do something

你会打网球吗？会。/ 不会。

B. Commenting on how well one does an activity

他打乒乓球打得很好。

STEP 3

ABOUT ONE'S DREAMS AND ASPIRATIONS

A. Stating one's dream job

你想当什么？我想当歌星。

B. Telling how often one does an activity

我天天唱歌。

217

àihào
你有什么爱好？
What are your hobbies?

yóuyǒng
我喜欢游泳。
I like swimming.

A Sports and games

生 词 NEW WORDS

生 词

NEW WORDS

爱好 n.	愛好	àihào	interest, hobbies
踢 v.		tī	to kick
打 v.		dǎ	to hit; to play a game

pǎobù
跑步 v.
to jog

yóuyǒng
游泳 v.
to swim

tī   zúqiú
踢足球 phr.

to play soccer

dǎ   lánqiú
打篮球 phr.
打籃球

to play basketball

dǎ   gǎnlǎnqiú
打橄榄球 phr.
打橄欖球

to play American football

dǎ   bàngqiú
打棒球 phr.

to play baseball

dǎ   pīngpāngqiú
打乒乓球 phr.

to play table tennis

dǎ   yǔmáoqiú
打羽毛球 phr.

to play badminton

dǎ   wǎngqiú
打网球 phr.
打網球

to play tennis

dǎ   tàijíquán
打太极拳 phr.
打太極拳

to do Taiji

dēng shān
登山 phr.

to go mountain climbing

huá xuě
滑雪 v.

to ski

You can ask people about their hobbies and interests using the question "你有什么爱好？" which means "What are your hobbies?"

The easiest way to answer is to use the verb 喜欢 (like) to say what you like doing.

Examples: ❶ 我喜欢踢足球。 I like playing soccer.
❷ 我喜欢打篮球。 I like to play basketball.

Note that for most ball games that involve the use of one or both hands, you use the verb 打 (e.g. 打棒球 and 打排球). But for soccer, you use the verb 踢 (kick) instead.

Conduct a survey to find out what your classmates' hobbies are. Record your findings in a chart similar to the one below. Then plot a graph to see which activities are most popular among students in your class.

Student A: 你有什么爱好？　　　Student B: 我喜欢……。

名字	爱好
马克	踢足球、游泳

 CULTURAL HIGHLIGHTS

Ping Pong Diplomacy

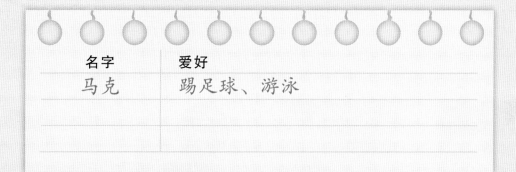

Table tennis, or ping pong, started to develop in China in the 1950s after Chairman Mao made a call for national exercise. Because it is a sport that requires simple equipment, it has flourished and becomes the most popular sport in China. Most of the world-class table tennis players hail from China, and in the past 50 years, the country has won countless awards from international table tennis competitions.

Table tennis was also instrumental in promoting diplomatic ties between China and the United States. In 1971, there was an exchange of table tennis players between China and the U.S. This helped thaw Sino-American relations and paved the way for U.S. President Richard Nixon's visit to Beijing in 1972.

你 的 爱 好 是 什 么 ？
What are your hobbies?

chànggē
我 的 爱 好 是 唱 歌 。
My hobby is singing.

生 词 NEW WORDS

tán gāngqín
弹 钢 琴 *phr.*
彈 鋼 琴
to play piano

xiàqí
下 棋 *phr.*
to play chess

xiě shūfǎ
写 书 法 *phr.*
寫 書 法
to practice calligraphy

huàhuà
画 画 *v.*
畫 畫
to draw

kànshū
看 书 *v.*
看 書
to read

xiězuò
写 作 *v.*
寫 作
to write

chànggē
唱 歌 *v.*
to sing

tiàowǔ
跳 舞 *v.*
to dance

LANGUAGE FOCUS

Another way of asking someone's interests and hobbies is 你的爱好是什么? Here, the reply statement follows the same word order by replacing 什么 with the answer.

Research online to find out what these famous people's hobbies or interests were when they were young. Work with your partner and use the following two speech patterns to talk about this topic.

Student A:

Garry Kasparov 有什么爱好？

Garry Kasparov 的爱好是什么？

Student B:

Garry Kasparov 喜欢……。

Garry Kasparov 的爱好是……。

Garry Kasparov

Condoleezza Rice

Madonna

Pablo Picasso

Mario Vargas Llosa

Yang Liping

Yao Ming

Lang Lang

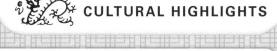

CULTURAL HIGHLIGHTS

The Four Traditional Arts of the Chinese Scholar

In ancient China, scholars were required to master the four arts: 琴 (qín), the playing of zither; 棋 (qí), the playing of *Weiqi*; 书 (shū), the practice of calligraphy; and 画 (huà), Chinese painting.

These arts provide the platform by which Chinese scholars demonstrate their strength in reasoning, creativity, expression and dexterity. Mastery of these arts fulfils the Chinese ideals of an educated man, who will then be considered "scholarly" or "a man of the arts."

ABOUT ONE'S ABILITIES AND SKILLS

你会打网球吗？
Can you play tennis?

我会打网球。
Yes, I can play tennis.

or

我不会打网球。
No, I can't play tennis.

A Asking about one's ability to do something

他会不会打太极拳？
Do you know how to play *Taiji*?

会 / 不会。
Yes./No.

生 词

NEW WORD

会 *aux. v.* | 會 | huì | can; be able to

LANGUAGE FOCUS

The model verb 会 is put before verbs to show capability. The negative form is 不会. To ask if someone knows how to do something, you can use either 会(verb)吗？ or 会不会(verb)？

You can answer with a simple 会 or 不会, or a statement that keeps the same word order as the question.

CULTURAL HIGHLIGHTS

Taiji

Taiji, as it is practiced in the West today, can perhaps be best thought of as a moving form of yoga and meditation combined. There are different forms or sets, and each consists of a sequence of movements. Many of these movements were originally derived from martial arts movements and perhaps even from the natural movements of animals and birds. However, the way they are performed in *Taiji* is slow, soft and graceful with smooth and even transitions between them.

1. Practice reading the following dialogs with a classmate. Replace the underlined words with those in the word bank for more practice.

❶ Student A: 你会下棋吗？
   Student B: 我会下棋。

> 弹钢琴　写书法　画画儿
> 打棒球　滑雪　　游泳

❷ Student A: 你会不会打篮球？
   Student B: 我会打篮球。

> 打太极拳　踢足球　游泳　跳舞
> 打乒乓球　打网球　下棋

2. Pretend you are organizing a class outing and need to pick one ball game that everyone can participate in. Come up with three options and conduct a survey to find out which of the three ball games is played by most, if not all, students in your class. Record your findings in the chart below.

> Student A: 你会……吗？　　Student B: 会／不会。

名字	棒球	橄榄球	网球
大卫	会	不会	会

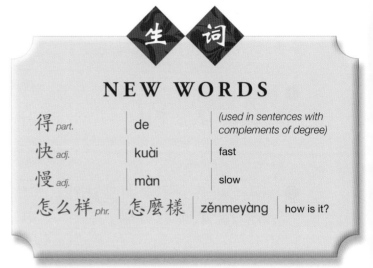

NEW WORDS

得 part.	de	(used in sentences with complements of degree)
快 adj.	kuài	fast
慢 adj.	màn	slow
怎么样 phr.	怎麼樣 zěnmeyàng	how is it?

de

他打篮球打得好吗?

Is he good at basketball?

他打篮球打得很好 / 打得不好。

He is very good at basketball./He is not so good at basketball.

zěnmeyàng

她游泳游得怎么样?

How well can she swim? (Is she a good swimmer?)

kuài

她游得很快。

She swims very fast. (She is a fast swimmer.)

or

màn

她游得很慢。

She cannot swim fast. (She is not a good swimmer.)

LANGUAGE FOCUS

得 is placed between a verb and a complement to show how well an action is being carried out, e.g. 打得很好.

With 得, there are three ways to ask and answer questions on how good a person's skills and abilities are. The first is to use the question word 吗. The second is to use the positive and negative forms of the adjective to form an affirmative-negative question. The third is to use 怎么样, which is placed at the end of the question, right after 得.

Examples:

❶ 你游得快吗?
Can you swim fast?

❷ 你游得快不快?
Can you swim fast?

❸ 你游得怎么样?
How well can you swim?

In reply, the answer follows the same word order as the question. The positive form has a degree adverb 很 added before the adjective, while the negative form places 不 before the adjective.

Examples:

❶ 我游得很快。
I can swim very fast.

❷ 我游得不快。
I cannot swim fast.

When the verb takes an object, the same verb will repeat again in the Verb + 得 + Complement structure.

Examples:

❶ 我弹钢琴弹得很好。
I can play the piano very well.

❷ 他打棒球打得不好。
He is not good at baseball.

1. Work with a classmate to ask and answer the following questions.

❶ 他打篮球打得好吗?

❷ 她打网球打得好不好?

❸ 马克踢足球踢得怎么样?

❹ 玛丽弹钢琴弹得好不好?

❺ 大卫打乒乓球打得怎么样?

❻ 安琪跳舞跳得好吗?

❼ 你奶奶打太极拳打得好不好?

❽ 他姐姐唱歌唱得好不好?

2. Below are three groups of words. Choose an appropriate one from each group to form questions and answers about one's skills and competencies.

Example: 她跳舞跳得怎么样? 她跳舞跳得很好。

打	踢	唱
跳	玩	弹
写		

羽毛球	网球	足球	歌
乒乓球	棒球	篮球	舞
太极拳	书法	钢琴	

好
快
慢

jiānglái xiǎng dāng

你将来想当什么?

What do you want to be in the future?

yùndòngyuán

我想当运动员。

I want to be an athlete.

A Stating one's dream job

生 词 NEW WORDS

gāngqínjiā

钢琴家 n.

鋼琴家

pianist

huàjiā

画家 n.

畫家

artist

zuòjiā

作家 n.

writer

gēshǒu

歌手 n.

singer

wǔdǎojiā

舞蹈家 n.

dancer

yùndòngyuán

运动员 n.

運動員

athlete

生 词 NEW WORDS

将来 n.	将來	jiānglái	in the future	律师 n.	律師	lùshī	lawyer
想 m.v.		xiǎng	to wish; to want	警察 n.		jǐngchá	policeman
当 v.	當	dāng	to be	厨师 n.	廚師	chúshī	chef
				记者 n.	記者	jìzhě	journalist
Extended				演员 n.	演員	yǎnyuán	actor
教师 n.	教師	jiàoshī	teacher	科学家 n.	科學家	kēxuéjiā	scientist
医生 n.	醫生	yīshēng	doctor				

To ask someone what he or she wants to be in the future, use "你将来想当什么?" 想 is a modal verb that expresses one's wish and is placed before the verb 当. In the answer, the word order is retained, and the answer is placed after the verb as the object.

Example:

你将来想当什么? 我想当画家。
What do you want to be in the future? I want to be an artist.

You can also form yes-no questions with 想, using either of the constructions 想……吗? or 想不想……?

Examples:

❶ 你将来想当钢琴家吗?
Do you want to be a pianist in the future?

❷ 你将来想不想当歌手?
Do you want to be a singer in the future?

The answer follows the same order as the question, with 想 for the affirmative reply and 不想 for the negative reply.

Ask at least five of your classmates what they want their profession(s) to be in the future. Follow the speech pattern and record your findings:

Student A: 你将来想当什么?   Student B: 我想当……。

Name	Dreams / Aspirations
芳芳	作家、记者

我天天打网球。
I play tennis every day.

měi

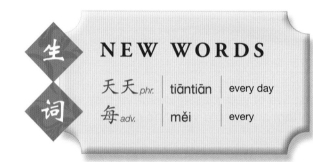

生	**NEW WORDS**		
词	天天 *phr.*	tiāntiān	every day
	每 *adv.*	měi	every

我每个星期二和星期四踢足球。
I play soccer every Tuesday and Thursday.

LANGUAGE FOCUS

One must work hard to realize one's dreams and aspirations. In order to do so, you need to develop the skills that the dream job or occupation requires. You also need to think about the frequency of practice or training.

天天 refers to frequency and can be used as an adverb in a sentence. It is followed by an action verb or verb phrase to indicate the activity and how frequently it takes place.

Examples:
❶ 我天天打乒乓球。
❷ 我天天跑步。
❸ 我天天游泳。

每 can also be used to express frequency. "每 + 个 + day of the week" forms an adverbial expression in a sentence to indicate which day in every week an activity takes place.

Examples:
❶ 我每个星期六游泳。
❷ 他每个星期一、三、五跑步。

The slight pause mark (、) in the above example is used to separate items listed in a series.

Try This!

1. Below is Mark's weekly schedule and it shows he is actively involved in sports. Study it and answer the following questions in Chinese.

星期天	星期一	星期二	星期三	星期四	星期五	星期六
跑步	跑步	跑步	跑步	跑步	跑步	跑步
踢足球	打篮球	打棒球	游泳	打篮球	踢足球	游泳

❶ On which days does Mark swim? _马克每个星期三和星期六游泳_。

❷ On which days does Mark play soccer? _____。

❸ On which days does he jog? _____。

❹ On which day does he play basketball? _____。

❺ On which day does he play baseball? _____。

2. Complete the sentences with the appropriate activities and frequency.

❶ 他想当篮球运动员，他天天_打篮球_。

❷ 他想当画家，他_____。

❸ 她想当舞蹈家，她_____。

❹ 她想当作家，她_____。

❺ 他想当钢琴家，他_____。

❻ 他想当足球运动员，他_____。

❼ 他想当歌手，他_____。

STEP 1
ABOUT ONE'S INTERESTS AND HOBBIES

Two students talking about their interests and hobbies

你有什么爱好？

　　我喜欢游泳，也喜欢唱歌。
我还喜欢打篮球、踢足球和打
网球。

　　你的爱好真多！

zhēn
really

你的爱好是什么？

　　我的爱好是弹钢琴。你呢？
我喜欢跳舞，还喜欢画画。

　　哈哈，我们都有
艺术细胞。

hā
sound of laughter

yìshù xìbāo
artistically inclined

STEP 2
ABOUT ONE'S ABILITIES AND SKILLS

Two students talking about a certain sport

你会打乒乓球吗？

　　不会，你会吗？
也不会。马克会打乒乓球。

　　他打乒乓球打得好吗？
他打得很好。

STEP 3
ABOUT ONE'S DREAMS AND ASPIRATIONS

One student telling another about his dream job and what he is doing to realize his dream

你喜欢跑步吗？

　　喜欢，我天天跑步。
你喜欢什么运动？

　　我喜欢打篮球。我每个星期
　　一、三、五都打篮球。
你将来想当篮球运动员吗？

　　对，我想当篮球运动员。
　　你呢？
我还没想好。　(I'm not sure yet.)

Step Up!

1. Each person takes a turn to act out his or her favorite hobby and have the class guess what it is. For example, if you like playing the piano, you can wiggle your fingers along an imaginary piano. If you like to paint, you can pretend to paint a picture with an imaginary brush. Make a list of everyone's hobby and put the information in your portfolio.

2. Research a famous person who shares the same interest or hobby that you do. Present what you have found to the class, and state whether you want to be like this person in the future.

3. Pick two sports that were contested in the most recent Olympics Games, and find out who were the gold medalists of these two sports events. Then present the following information to the class:

List the following information for sports that interest you:

* Two sports contested at the Olympic Games
* Names of the two gold medalists
* Their ages and nationalities
* Their skills
* How frequently they trained

4. Find out from at least five classmates how often and how much time they spend on their hobbies. Record your findings in a chart.

Name	Interests / Hobbies	Frequency
马克	踢足球	天天
	打网球	每个星期一和星期三

Fun Time!

Below are some popular extracurricular activities that middle schools in China offer. Choose one or more that may interest you and explain why.

Sports and Games

羽毛球
Badminton

乒乓球
Table tennis

篮球
Basketball

wǔshù
武术
Wushu (martial arts)

Which **activity** do you like?

The Arts and Music

Zhōngguó yuèqì
中国乐器
Chinese instrument

xiàng
中国象棋
Chinese chess

中国书法
Chinese calligraphy

中国画
Chinese painting

wéi
围棋
Chinese Go

I have learned...

Core Vocabulary

爱好 *n.*	爱好	àihào	interest, hobbies	写作 *v.*	寫作	xiězuò	to write
踢 *v.*		tī	to kick	唱歌 *v.*		chànggē	to sing
打 *v.*		dǎ	to hit; to play a game	跳舞 *v.*		tiàowǔ	to dance
跑步 *v.*		pǎobù	to jog	会 *aux.v.*	會	huì	can; be able to
游泳 *v.*		yóuyǒng	to swim	得 *part.*		de	*(used in sentences with complements of degree)*
足球 *n.*		zúqiú	soccer	快 *adj.*		kuài	fast
乒乓球 *n.*		pīngpāngqiú	table tennis	慢 *adj.*		màn	slow
篮球 *n.*	籃球	lánqiú	basketball	怎么样 *phr.*	怎麼樣	zěnmeyàng	how is it?
网球 *n.*	網球	wǎngqiú	tennis	将来 *n.*	將來	jiānglái	in the future
羽毛球 *n.*		yǔmáoqiú	badminton	想 *m.v.*		xiǎng	to wish; to want
橄榄球 *n.*	橄欖球	gǎnlǎnqiú	American football	当 *v.*	當	dāng	to be
棒球 *n.*		bàngqiú	baseball	钢琴家 *n.*	鋼琴家	gāngqínjiā	pianist
登山 *v.*		dēng shān	to go mountain climbing	画家 *n.*	畫家	huàjiā	artist
太极拳 *n.*	太極拳	tàijíquán	*Taiji*	作家 *n.*		zuòjiā	writer
滑雪 *v.*	滑雪	huá xuè	to ski	歌手 *n.*		gēshǒu	singer
弹钢琴 *phr.*		tán gāngqín	to play piano	舞蹈家 *n.*		wǔdǎojiā	dancer
下棋 *phr.*		xiàqí	to play chess	运动员 *n.*	運動員	yùndòngyuán	athlete
写书法 *phr.*	寫書法	xiě shūfǎ	to practice calligraphy	天天 *phr.*		tiāntiān	every day
画画 *v.*	畫畫	huàhuà	to draw	每 *adv.*		měi	every
看书 *v.*	看書	kànshū	to read				

Extended Vocabulary

教师 *n.*	教師	jiàoshī	teacher	厨师 *n.*	厨師	chúshī	chef
医生 *n.*	醫生	yīshēng	doctor	记者 *n.*	記者	jìzhě	journalist
律师 *n.*	律師	lǜshī	lawyer	演员 *n.*	演員	yǎnyuán	actor
警察 *n.*		jǐngchá	policeman	科学家 *n.*	科學家	kēxuéjiā	scientist

233

SENTENCE PATTERNS

你有什么爱好？我喜欢游泳。

你的爱好是什么？我的爱好是唱歌。

你会打网球吗？我会打网球。我不会打网球。

他会不会打太极拳？会／不会。

他打篮球打得好吗？他打篮球打得很好／打得不好。

她游泳游得怎么样？她游得很快。／她游得很慢。

你想当什么？我想当运动员。

我天天打网球。我每个星期二和星期四踢足球。

I can do!

Interpretive Communication

❑ I can understand when someone tells me about his or her interests or hobbies.

❑ I can understand when someone tells me what he or she is good at.

❑ I can understand when someone talks about his or her dream job.

❑ I can understand when someone talks about how much time is spent on his or her hobbies.

Interpersonal Communication

❑ I can exchange information about interests and hobbies

❑ I can ask and answer questions about someone's abilities.

❑ I can ask and answer questions about dream jobs/professions.

❑ I can exchange information about time spent on hobbies.

Presentational Communication

❑ I can talk about my interests and hobbies.

❑ I can comment on how well one does an activity.

❑ I can state my dream job.

❑ I can tell how often and how much time I spend on my hobbies.

Cultural Knowledge

❑ I can relate the history of table tennis, how it started and its role in restoring China-U.S. relations in the 1970s.

❑ I can state the four main accomplishments required of the Chinese scholar.

❑ I can talk about the origin and the key characteristics of *Taiji*.

It tastes so good!

好吃！

COMMUNICATIVE GOALS

◆ Talking about foods and beverages

◆ Describing the taste of various foods

◆ Expressing food preferences

◆ Asking choice-type questions

◆ Ordering food

Cultural Knowledge

◆ Fruits grown in China

◆ Popular Chinese dishes and beverages

◆ Fast-food in China

◆ History of chopsticks

◆ Food symbolism in Chinese culture

◆ Order of courses in a Chinese meal

Get ready...

Look at the following pictures of fruits and vegetables. Decide if they are normally grown and/or eaten in China, America, or both countries. An item may be eaten in one country but comes from another country.

Complete the chart below. If you know in which part/state/province of the country the fruit or vegetable is generally grown, write that in the space. Compare your answers with a classmate's.

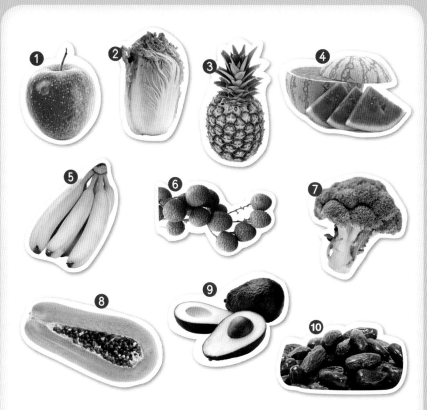

Fruits and Vegetables	China		U.S.		State / Province
	Grown	Eaten	Grown	Eaten	
❶ Apple					
❷ Chinese cabbage					
❸ Pineapple					
❹ Watermelon					
❺ Banana					
❻ Lychee					
❼ Broccoli					
❽ Papaya					
❾ Avocado					
❿ Red date					

STEPS *at a glance!*

TALKING ABOUT FOODS AND HOW THEY TASTE

A. Asking what food one is having

你吃什么? 我吃饺子。

你喝什么? 我喝茶。

B. Asking if the food one is having tastes good

面包好吃吗? 面包很好吃。

可乐好喝吗? 可乐很好喝。

C. Describing the taste of foods

西瓜很甜。咖啡很苦。

EXPRESSING FOOD PREFERENCES

A. Stating the foods one likes or dislikes

我喜欢吃饺子，也喜欢吃热狗。

我最喜欢吃鱼。我最不喜欢吃沙拉。

B. Asking what foods one wants to eat or drink

你要吃什么? 我要吃炒饭。

你要喝什么? 我要喝果汁。

C. Asking choice–type questions

你要吃饺子还是油条?

ORDERING FOOD

A. Measure words for food dishes

一碗面，两杯茶。

B. Ordering food

你要点什么菜?

来两个包子，再来一碗面。

237

COMMON FOOD ITEMS

Vegetables

shēngcài 生菜 lettuce	bōcài 菠菜 spinach
xīlánhuā 西兰花 broccoli	qíncài 芹菜 celery
yùmǐ 玉米 corn	báicài 白菜 Chinese cabbage
fānqié 番茄 tomato	làjiāo 辣椒 chili pepper

Meats

jīròu 鸡肉 chicken	zhūròu 猪肉 pork
niúròu 牛肉 beef	yángròu 羊肉 mutton

Seafood

yú 鱼 fish	xiā 虾 prawn

Fruit

píngguǒ 苹果 apple	chéngzi 橙子 orange
xiāngjiāo 香蕉 banana	cǎoméi 草莓 strawberry
xīguā 西瓜 watermelon	pútao 葡萄 grape

Dairy Products

niúnǎi
牛奶
milk

huángyóu
黄油
butter

nǎilào
奶酪
cheese

Common Food Items

Before you start learning the speech patterns for foods, it would be good to know the Chinese names of the most common Chinese and Western food items of the modern day.

Condiment

táng 糖 sugar	hújiāofěn 胡椒粉 pepper
fānqiéjiàng 番茄酱 ketchup	yán 盐 salt

Others

jīdàn
鸡蛋
egg

dòufu
豆腐
beancurd

COMMON CHINESE FOODS

Staples

mǐfàn	miàntiáo
米饭	面条
rice	noodle

Snacks

yóutiáo	bāozi
油条	包子
fried dough stick	meat or vegetable bun
mántou	guōtiē
馒头	锅贴
bun	pan-fried dumpling
jiǎozi	chūnjuǎn
饺子	春卷
dumpling	spring roll

Soups

húntuntāng
馄饨汤
wanton soup
suānlàtāng
酸辣汤
hot and sour soup
dànhuātāng
蛋花汤
egg drop soup

Rice Dishes

dànchǎofàn	Yángzhōuchǎofàn
蛋炒饭	扬州炒饭
egg fried rice	Yangzhou fried rice

Noodles Dishes

sùchǎomiàn	hǎixiānchǎomiàn
素炒面	海鲜炒面
vegetarian fried noodles	seafood fried noodles

Porridge Dishes

huāshēngzhōu	yúzhōu
花生粥	鱼粥
peanut porridge	fish porridge

Beverages

Zhōngguóchá
中国茶
Chinese tea
dòujiāng
豆浆
soybean milk

Main Dishes

tángcùpáigǔ	Běijīng kǎoyā	zhēngyú
糖醋排骨	北京烤鸭	蒸鱼
sweet and sour pork	Peking duck	steamed fish
gōngbǎo jīdīng	mápó dòufu	yúxiāng ròusī
宫保鸡丁	麻婆豆腐	鱼香肉丝
spicy chicken	spicy beancurd	shredded pork in spicy sauce

Desserts

hóngdòutāng
红豆汤
red bean soup
zhīma tāngyuán
芝麻汤圆
dumpling with sesame filling

COMMON WESTERN FOODS

BREAKFAST

miànbāo 面包 bread	màipiàn 麦片 cereal	chǎodàn 炒蛋 scrambled eggs	hōngdòu 烘豆 baked beans	xiánròu 咸肉 bacon
huǒtuǐ 火腿 ham	xiāngcháng 香肠 sausage			
kāfēi 咖啡 coffee	chá 茶 tea			
guǒzhī 果汁 fruit juice	guǒjiàng 果酱 jam			

LUNCH / DINNER

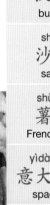

hànbǎo 汉堡 burger	règǒu 热狗 hotdog	jīpái 鸡排 chicken fillet
shālā 沙拉 salad	sānmíngzhì 三明治 sandwich	yángpái 羊排 lamb chop
shǔtiáo 薯条 French fries	pīsà 披萨 pizza	niúpái 牛排 steak
yìdàlìmiàn 意大利面 spaghetti	fānqiétāng 番茄汤 tomato soup	zhūpái 猪排 pork chop

DRINKS / DESSERTS

kělè 可乐 cola	dàngāo 蛋糕 cake
bīngqílín 冰淇淋 ice-cream	

STEP UP WITH CHINESE • 成长

TALKING ABOUT FOODS AND HOW THEY TASTE

chī
你 吃 什 么 ?
What are you eating?

我 吃 饺 子 。
I am having dumplings.

A Asking what food one is having

hē
你 喝 什 么 ?
What are you drinking?

我 喝 茶 。
I am having tea.

生 词

NEW WORDS

| 吃 v. | chī | to eat |
| 喝 v. | hē | to drink |

LANGUAGE FOCUS

To ask what food one is having, you use the verb 吃/喝 with 什么 to form a question. To answer the question, simply replace 什么 with the name of the food item.

Examples: ❶ 你吃什么？我吃蛋炒饭。 What are you eating? I am having egg fried rice.
❷ 他喝什么？他喝豆浆。 What is he drinking? He is drinking soybean milk.

 CULTURAL HIGHLIGHTS

Three Meals a Day

In China, people generally do not eat fruit for breakfast, and breakfast usually consists of deep-fried dough sticks (油条 yóutiáo), a soybean drink, pancakes, eggs, and porridge. Generally lunch is a big meal, so it often contains many different dishes, and it is usually eaten around noon. For dinner, Chinese people usually do not eat much. There is a Chinese saying that goes like this:

Zǎofàn chī de hǎo, zhōngfàn chī de bǎo, wǎnfàn chī de shǎo.
早饭吃得好， 中饭吃得饱， 晚饭吃得少。

It means that one should have a good breakfast, a heavy lunch, and a light dinner. However, in contemporary times, it is not always easy to practice this custom given the hectic, busy urban life.

1. **Challenge Yourself:** Put the following foods into the correct categories. You may refer to the chart of Common Chinese Foods.

mápó dòufu	**❶** 麻婆豆腐
gōngbǎo jīdīng	**❷** 宫保鸡丁
Zhōngguóchá	**❸** 中国茶
suānlàtāng	**❹** 酸辣汤
dòujiāng	**❺** 豆浆
zhīma tāngyuán	**❻** 芝麻汤圆
Běijīng kǎoyā	**❼** 北京烤鸭
huāshēngzhōu	**❽** 花生粥
dànhuātāng	**❾** 蛋花汤
chǎofàn	**❿** 炒饭

吃

喝

2. Look at the following pictures of food and practice asking and answering questions with a classmate. Follow the pattern:

Student A: 他吃 / 喝什么？　　Student B: 他吃 / 喝……。

chǎofàn
炒饭

guōtiē
锅贴

Zhōngguóchá
中国茶

Běijīng kǎoyā
北京烤鸭

zhēngyú
蒸鱼

bāozi
包子

dòujiāng
豆浆

yóutiáo
油条

zhīma tāngyuán
芝麻汤圆

húntuntāng
馄饨汤

面包 好吃 吗？
How's the bread?

面包 很 好吃。
It's good.

可乐 好 喝 吗？
How's the coke?

可乐 很 好喝。
It's nice.

NEW WORDS

| 好吃 *phr.* | hǎochī | tasty; delicious (*used for food*) |
| 好喝 *phr.* | hǎohē | tasty; delicious (*used for drinks*) |

◆ LANGUAGE FOCUS

To ask someone how they find their food or drink, you can form a question using the adjective 好吃/好喝 with the interrogative particle 吗.

Examples:

❶ 披萨好吃吗？ How's the pizza?

❷ 果汁好喝吗？ How's the fruit juice?

To say that the food tastes good, simply retain the word order and drop the particle 吗. Positive Chinese adjectives usually need an adverb. If no other adverb is used, the adjective is preceded with 很, which means "very." In this situation, however, 很 does not necessarily carry any meaning.

Examples:

❶ 披萨很好吃。
The pizza tastes good (or tastes very good).

❷ 果汁很好喝。
The juice tastes good (or tastes very good).

If you simply don't like how the food or drink tastes, you can answer 不好吃 or 不好喝.

Examples:

❶ 披萨好吃吗？ 不好吃。
How's the pizza? Not very nice.

❷ 果汁好喝吗？ 不好喝。
How's the fruit juice? Not very nice.

Try This!

1. Work with a classmate to practice the following speech pattern using the pictures below. Give a negative reply for those pictures that are marked with an "✗."

Student A:
……好吃/好喝吗?

Student B:
……很好吃/好喝 or ……不好吃/不好喝。

niúnǎi
牛奶

miànbāo
面包

hànbǎo
汉堡 ✗

kāfēi
咖啡

dàngāo
蛋糕 ✗

kělè
可乐

pīsà
披萨

shǔtiáo
薯条

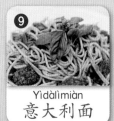
Yìdàlìmiàn
意大利面

niúpái
牛排 ✗

2. Conduct a survey to find out what food sold in your school cafeteria is popular among students in your class. Draw up a list of foods and drinks sold in the cafeteria and ask at least 10 of your classmates how they find each food item. Record your findings. Use the following speech pattern and chart as your guide.

Student A: 汉堡好吃吗?
Student B: 很好吃。

Student A: 果汁好喝吗?
Student B: 不好喝。

名字	汉堡	果汁
大卫	好吃	不好喝

 CULTURAL HIGHLIGHTS

Western Fast-Food in China

Western fast-food restaurants like McDonald's (麦当劳, Màidāngláo), Kentucky Fried Chicken (肯德鸡, Kěndéjī), and Pizza Hut (必胜客, Bìshèngkè) are nothing new in Chinese cities. They are especially popular among children and office workers and have gained a place in the food industry in China.

Two factors have contributed to their success. One is a good dining environment. Western style dining tables and chairs, utensils, and flavors, plus ice cream and coca cola drinks, all bring a sense of novelty to young people and children. The second factor is the convenience and quick service in these restaurants. Since lunch time for office workers is often limited, these restaurants have become a natural choice for quick food.

Psychologically, Western style food is popular in China because it has met the needs of young people who want to pursue new experiences. But most Chinese people still prefer Chinese style food. For Chinese people who prefer rich and varied food, Western style fast-food has its limitations because they feel that fast-foods lack the gourmet flavors of traditional Chinese food.

C Describing the taste of foods

suān

葡萄很酸。

The grapes are sour.

tián

西瓜很甜。

The watermelon is sweet.

kǔ

咖啡很苦。

The coffee is bitter.

là

汤很辣。

The soup is spicy.

xián

咸肉很咸。

The bacon is salty.

dàn

粥很淡。

The porridge is bland.

NEW WORDS

生 词

酸 adj.	suān	sour	辣 adj.		là	spicy
甜 adj.	tián	sweet	咸 adj.	鹹	xián	salty
苦 adj.	kǔ	bitter	淡 adj.		dàn	bland

LANGUAGE FOCUS

Sometimes, it may not be enough to just say that the food tastes good (好吃) or not good (不好吃). The taste-related adjectives introduced in this section allow you to be more specific about how food tastes.

Chinese adjectives are placed after the nouns they describe. As all Chinese adjectives implicitly include "to be," the verb 是 is not needed. So instead of saying *西瓜是很甜 (The watermelon is very sweet), you say 西瓜很甜.

To form negative adjectives, place 不 before the adjective, as in 西瓜不甜 (The watermelon is not sweet).

1. Look at the following pictures of food and state what you think their tastes are.

苦

酸　甜　苦　辣　咸　淡

chá
茶

dàngāo
蛋糕

làjiāo
辣椒

pútao
葡萄

nǎilào
奶酪

tāng
汤

cǎoméi
草莓

kāfēi
咖啡

suānlàtāng
酸辣汤

bīngqílín
冰淇淋

2. Tell your classmate what you ate for breakfast. Use adjectives to describe the taste of the foods you had. Then let your classmate describe his/her breakfast to you. See the example on the right.

早上我吃三明治了，三明治很好吃。我还吃水果了。西瓜很甜，橙子很酸。我也喝咖啡了，很苦。

 CULTURAL HIGHLIGHTS

Chopsticks

Chopsticks (筷子, kuàizi) are typically 9 to 10 inches long and have square cross-section ends that taper to tips having a round cross-section.

It is believed that the first chopsticks were developed over 5000 years ago in China. Early Asian man would retrieve his food from the fire using sticks or branches broken from trees. Later, as the population grew and resources became scarce, people would cut food into smaller pieces to save fuel because the smaller portions cooked faster. This eliminated the need for knives, and chopsticks became the utensil of choice.

Confucius probably helped to promote the use of chopsticks because he believed that the honorable and upright man "allows no knives on his table." His teachings probably increased the popularity of using chopsticks. Centuries later, chopsticks spread from China to other countries in Asia.

It has been said that using chopsticks improves memory, increases finger dexterity, and can be useful in learning and improving skills such as Chinese character writing and brush painting.

我喜欢吃饺子，
I like dumplings,

不喜欢吃热狗。
but not hotdogs.

A Stating the foods one likes or dislikes

我最喜欢吃鱼，
I like fish most.

最不喜欢吃沙拉。
I like salad least.

Try This!

1. Tell your classmate whether you like the following foods or not. Use 最 for the ones that you like most or least.

   hànbǎo
   ❶ 汉堡
   burger

   shǔtiáo
   ❷ 薯条
   French fries

   pīsà
   ❸ 披萨
   pizza

   Yìdàlìmiàn
   ❹ 意大利面
   spaghetti

   dàngāo
   ❺ 蛋糕
   cake

   kělè
   ❻ 可乐
   coke

   jiǎozi
   ❼ 饺子
   dumplings

   chūnjuǎn
   ❽ 春卷
   spring roll

   tángcùpáigǔ
   ❾ 糖醋排骨
   sweet and sour pork

   Zhōngguóchá
   ❿ 中国茶
   Chinese tea

2. Ask at least 10 classmates what their favorite foods and drinks are. Then make two charts to determine the most popular foods and drinks.

   Student A:
   你喜欢吃什么？
   你喜欢喝什么？

   Student B:
   我喜欢吃……
   我喜欢喝……

 **CULTURAL HIGHLIGHTS**

The Significance of Fish

Do you know that Chinese people like to eat fish? Fish is delicious and nourishing. In addition, fish is also considered to be auspicious, because "fish" in Chinese (鱼, yú) shares the same pronunciation with another Chinese character 余 which means "surplus."

There is a Chinese expression 年年有余 (nián nián yǒu yú) which means "May there be a surplus every year." Since the pronunciation of the word for surplus is the same as the word for fish, during the Chinese New Year and during festivals, fish is always found on the dinner table, as a symbol of hope for abundance and surplus every year.

yào
你要吃什么？
What do you want to eat?

我要吃炒饭。
I want (to eat) fried rice.

你要喝什么？
What do you want to drink?

我要喝果汁。
I want (to drink) fruit juice.

生 词
NEW WORD

要 *v. / aux. v.* | yào | to want

LANGUAGE FOCUS

要 is used to express one's wishes. It can serve as a verb or an auxiliary verb.

When used as a verb, it is placed before the noun or pronoun:

❶ 你要什么？我要饺子。 What do you want? I want dumplings.

❷ 他要什么？他要春卷。 What does he want? He wants spring rolls.

When used as an auxiliary verb, it is placed before the main verb:

❶ 你要吃什么？我要吃汉堡。 What do you want to eat? I want (to eat) a burger.

❷ 她要喝什么？她要喝中国茶。 What does she want to drink? She wants (to drink) Chinese tea.

To answer in the negative to a 吗 question or a positive/negative question, you use 不想 which means "don't want."

Examples:

❶ 你要吃披萨吗？我不想吃披萨。 Do you want to eat pizza? No, I don't want (to eat) pizza.

❷ 你要喝咖啡吗？我不想喝咖啡。 Do you want to drink coffee (or not) ? No, I don't want (to drink) coffee.

DO YOU KNOW . . .
你知道吗？

There are many drink stands in the streets of big Chinese cities such as Beijing. If you want to know what people in China are drinking today, you can go to one of the stands and watch what people order. Chinese people do not only drink tea, for almost all kinds of drinks from all over the world can be ordered there. Milk has become a common drink for Chinese people today due to the influence of Western countries.

Coca Cola was probably the earliest Western drink to enter the Chinese market and now Coca Cola, Pepsi, Seven-up, and Sprite can be found in most Chinese supermarkets and restaurants.

1. Make up answers to the following questions using the food names you have learned.

   ❶ 安琪要吃什么？ ⟶ 安琪要吃炒饭。　❻ 姐姐要喝什么？

   ❷ 大卫要喝什么？　❼ 弟弟要吃什么？

   ❸ 爸爸要吃什么？　❽ 妹妹要喝什么？

   ❹ 妈妈要喝什么？　❾ 李叔叔要吃什么？

   ❺ 哥哥要吃什么？　❿ 王阿姨要喝什么？

2. Pretend you have to buy food and drinks from the school cafeteria for five of your classmates. Ask your classmates what they want, and write them on a piece of paper.

   Student A: 你要吃什么？　Student B: 我要吃……

   Student A: 你要喝什么？　Student B: 我要喝……

3. Your class is planning an end-of-semester party. You are part of the organizing committee responsible for food. You have drawn up a list consisting of Chinese and Western foods, but you are not sure if it will be well received by the class. Conduct a survey to find out what your classmates think of the proposed food items. Use the following speech patterns and record their responses in the chart below.

   Student A: 你要吃/喝……吗？　Student B: 要/不要。

	饺子	春卷	披萨	汉堡
马克	要	不要	不要	要
安琪	要	要	要	不要

生 词

NEW WORD

还是 *conj.* | 還是 | háishì | or

háishì

① 你喜欢吃炒饭还是炒面？
Do you like fried rice or fried noodles?

② 你要喝什么？
What do you want to drink?

咖啡还是茶？
Coffee or tea?

LANGUAGE FOCUS

Choice-type questions present a person with two or more choices and he or she answers by choosing one of the options. 还是 is used to separate the choices in the question. When there are three or more choices, 还是 is placed before the last choice.

Examples:
你喜欢吃汉堡还是披萨？
Do you like burgers or pizzas?

你要喝可乐、果汁还是豆浆？
Do you want coke, fruit juice or soybean milk?

Another way to ask a choice-type question is to break it up into two smaller questions. The first question asks what the person wants to eat/drink using 什么. The second follows up by offering some choices.

Examples:
你喜欢吃什么？汉堡还是披萨？
What do you like to eat? Burgers or pizzas?

你要喝什么？可乐、果汁还是豆浆？
What do you want to drink? Coke, fruit juice or soybean milk?

DO **YOU** KNOW . . .
你知道吗？

Fruits symbolize different things in different cultures. Apples are healthy and we even have a saying, "An apple a day keeps the doctor away." There are some customs on how to eat certain fruits. For example, in China a couple should never cut a pear in half and share it. The peach is a symbol for longevity in China, while oranges and apples make great gifts.

Why are these so? Find out the symbolism of these fruits and others and share your findings with the rest of the class.

1. Make choice-type questions with the given food items as choices. You may use 喜欢 or 要 in the questions.

　　　mǐfàn　　miàntiáo
❶ 米饭 / 面条 ⟶ 你喜欢吃米饭还是面条?
　　rice / noodle
　　　　　　　　　　　　or
　　　　　　　⟶ 你要吃什么? 米饭还是面条?

　　jiǎozi　shǔtiáo
❷ 饺子 / 薯条
dumpling / French fries

　　kāfēi　chá
❸ 咖啡 / 茶
coffee / tea

　　niúnǎi　　dòujiāng
❹ 牛奶 / 豆浆
milk / soybean milk

　　niúpái　yángpái　zhūpái
❺ 牛排 / 羊排 / 猪排
steak / lamb chop / pork chop

　　règǒu　chūnjuǎn
❻ 热狗 / 春卷
hotdog / spring roll

　　píngguǒ　cǎoméi　　pútao
❼ 苹果 / 草莓 / 葡萄
apple / strawberry / grapes

　　tāngyuán　dàngāo
❽ 汤圆 / 蛋糕
dumpling / cake

　　yóutiáo　miànbāo
❾ 油条 / 面包
dough sticks / bread

　　suānlàtāng　　fānqiétāng　　húntuntāng
❿ 酸辣汤 / 番茄汤 / 馄饨汤
hot and sour soup / tomato soup / wanton soup

2. Choose three fruits and three vegetables from the list you learned earlier. Then draw up a table like the one below. Use it to ask at least five classmates which of the three fruits (or vegetables) they like to eat using choice-type questions. Put a check under the food item they like.

Student A: 你喜欢吃…、…还是…?　　Student B: 我喜欢吃……。

	苹果	橙子	西瓜	生菜	菠菜	西兰花
大卫	✔					

3. Role-play a scenario in which a flight attendant serves in-flight meal to a passenger. See the example dialog below and make one up with a classmate.

Ⓐ 你要吃什么? 鸡排还是三明治?

Ⓑ 鸡排。

Ⓐ 你要喝什么? 咖啡还是茶?

Ⓑ 我要咖啡, 谢谢。

　　　bú kèqi
Ⓐ 不客气。
(Don't mention it.)

Before you learn how to order dishes from a Chinese menu, it is necessary to know the measure words for common menu dishes, as you normally have to state the quantity of the items you are ordering. Below are some common measure words for different types of dishes.

A Measure words for food dishes

生 词
NEW WORDS

wǎn
碗 m.w.
(used for dishes served in bowls)

pán
盘 m.w.
盤
(used for dishes served on plates)

dié
碟 m.w.
(used for dishes served on small plates)

fèn
份 m.w.
(used for dishes that come in portions or servings)

kuài
块 m.w.
塊
(used for cakes and pastries)

bēi
杯 m.w.
(used for drinks served in cups)

píng
瓶 m.w.
(used for bottled drinks)

guàn
罐 m.w.
(used for drinks in a can)

gè
个 m.w.
個
(used for general food items)

Try This!

1. Fill in the blanks with the appropriate measure words.

① 一_____ chǎofàn 炒饭
fried rice

② 三_____ guǒzhī 果汁
fruit juice

③ 五_____ dàngāo 蛋糕
cake

④ 两_____ shālā 沙拉
salad

⑤ 一_____ sānmíngzhì 三明治
sandwich

⑥ 四_____ fānqiétāng 番茄汤
tomato soup

⑦ 三_____ yángpái 羊排
lamb chop

⑧ 两_____ kělè 可乐
coke

⑨ 五_____ miànbāo 面包
bread

⑩ 四_____ shǔtiáo 薯条
French fries

2. Describe the following pictures using the correct measure words and food names.

三个披萨

①
pīsà
披萨

②
kāfēi
咖啡

③
húntuntāng
馄饨汤

④
mápó dòufu
麻婆豆腐

⑤
suāntián páigǔ
酸甜排骨

⑥
guǒzhī
果汁

⑦
huāshēngzhōu
花生粥

⑧
Běijīng kǎoyā
北京烤鸭

diǎn

Ⓐ 我们点菜。
We are ready to order.

Ⓑ 好的，你们要点什么菜？
OK, what dishes would you like?

lái   *zài*

Ⓐ 来两个包子，再来一碗面。
Two meat buns and a bowl of noodles.

Ⓒ 我要一盘饺子。
Give me a plate of dumplings.

NEW WORDS 生词

点 v.	點	diǎn	to order
来 v.	來	lái	to bring; send
再 adv.		zài	again, another

LANGUAGE FOCUS

In this section, you will learn some basic statements to help you order food in a Chinese restaurant. To order food is 点菜. Once you have looked over the menu (菜单 càidān), you can use one of the following sentences to tell the waiter you are ready:

我们点菜。   We are ready to order.
我们要/想点菜。   We wish to order.

In response, the waiter will ask you what dishes you want to order using a 什么 (what) question:

你们要点什么菜？
What would you like to order?

You can reply with the verb 要 or 来 (in colloquial Chinese) which means "to bring here." You will need to use the measure words from the previous section to specify the quantities you are ordering. To add a different dish to your last order, use 还要 or 再来 (to bring another).

我要两个包子，还要一碗面。
I'd like two buns and a bowl of noodles.

来两个包子，再来一碗面。
Bring us two buns and a bowl of noodles.

1. Below is a dialog between four patrons and a waitress at a restaurant. Complete the dialog using the new words learned in this section and the appropriate measure words.

Ⓐ 小姐，我们＿＿点＿菜。

Ⓑ 你们要＿＿＿什么菜？

Ⓐ ＿＿＿一碟春卷，＿＿＿来一＿＿＿酸辣汤。

Ⓒ 我＿＿＿一＿＿＿炒饭。

Ⓓ 我＿＿＿一个糖醋排骨，＿＿＿要一碗饭。

Ⓔ ＿＿＿一只北京烤鸭。

Ⓑ 你们要什么饮料？
yǐnliào
beverage

Ⓐ 来一＿＿＿中国茶。

Ⓒ 可乐。

Ⓓ 果汁。

Ⓔ 我也＿＿＿一＿＿＿可乐。

2. Practice reading the above dialog with four other classmates. Then make one up with them and present it to the class.

CULTURAL HIGHLIGHTS

Order of Courses

The order of courses in Chinese cuisine is somewhat different from that in Western cuisine. When eating in a Chinese restaurant, a variety of small, cold dishes are often served first. Then come the hot dishes which are bigger in portion. Soup is served after the hot dishes, followed by rice or noodles. Desserts are served at the end. Drinks like Chinese tea, soft drinks, juices and liquor are served throughout the meal. Usually, the foods are prepared as common dishes to be shared among the table of family or friends. Thus, they are mainly consumed communally.

A Western meal consists of three to four courses: soup, salad, main course, dessert. Coffee and tea are usually served after the meal. Each of the courses is prepared in individual portions, different from the Chinese communal dishes.

STEP 1
TALKING ABOUT FOODS AND HOW THEY TASTE

Two students in the classroom talking about lunch just now

你午饭吃什么了?
　　我吃蛋炒饭了,还喝酸辣汤了。
蛋炒饭好吃吗?
　　很好吃。
酸辣汤呢?
　　很辣。你吃什么了?
我吃饺子了。

Two students talking about the fruits they are eating

你的西瓜甜吗?
　　很甜,很好吃。你的葡萄呢?
有点酸,不过还好。
　　哦,给你一片西瓜。
谢谢!

STEP 2
EXPRESSING FOOD PREFERENCES

Two students at the school cafeteria discussing the fruits and drinks to order

你要吃什么水果?苹果还是橙子?
　　我要吃橙子。
你喝咖啡吗?
　　我不喝咖啡,咖啡很苦。
我也是,我喜欢喝果汁。
　　我也喜欢喝果汁,还喜欢喝汽水。
我们都喜欢喝甜的。

STEP 3
ORDERING FOOD

Ordering food in a Chinese restaurant

您点菜吗?这是菜单。
　　来个麻婆豆腐。
　　　　我要个西兰花。
　　再来只北京烤鸭。
　　　　好!北京烤鸭很好吃。
　　再来两盘饺子。
你们喝什么?
　　来一瓶可乐。
　　　　我要中国茶,谢谢。

Step Up!

1. Read the following passage about three friends having lunch together. Then fill out the chart with the foods they had that day at the restaurant.

> 安琪和马克中午十二点半在餐馆 (cānguǎn, restaurant) 吃午饭，安琪要披萨和可乐，马克要汉堡和可乐。他们的朋友芳芳一点钟来餐馆，她要吃热狗和沙拉，还要喝果汁。安琪和芳芳都喜欢吃蛋糕，马克喜欢吃冰淇淋。

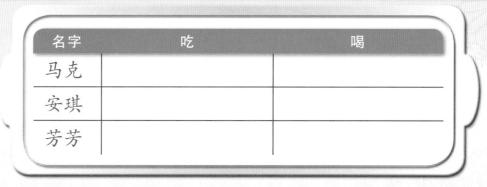

名字	吃	喝
马克		
安琪		
芳芳		

2. You plan to prepare a simple dinner for your family. Pick three Chinese or Western dishes that you think your family will enjoy. Then draw up a grocery list by writing down the ingredients you need for each of the three dishes. Present your dinner menu to the class. Include the name and ingredients of each dish.

Dish 1 Ingredients
_____
_____
_____

Dish 2 Ingredients
_____
_____
_____

Dish 3 Ingredients
_____
_____
_____

3. A local Chinese restaurant is having a set lunch promotion, featuring a bowl of soup, one main course, a dessert and a drink. Below is the restaurant menu. With a classmate, role-play the scenario in which a patron orders a set lunch from the waiter/waitress at this restaurant. Present your dialog to the class.

MENU   SET LUNCH @ $15

Main course
扬州炒饭
海鲜炒面
糖醋排骨 + 米饭

Soup
酸辣汤
馄饨汤
蛋花汤

Drink
可乐
果汁
中国茶

Dessert
红豆汤   芝麻汤圆   水果

Fun Time!

The food pyramid provides nutritional guidelines on the amount of food to consume each day for each food category. Fill in the food categories in the pyramid below with the names of foods you have learned.

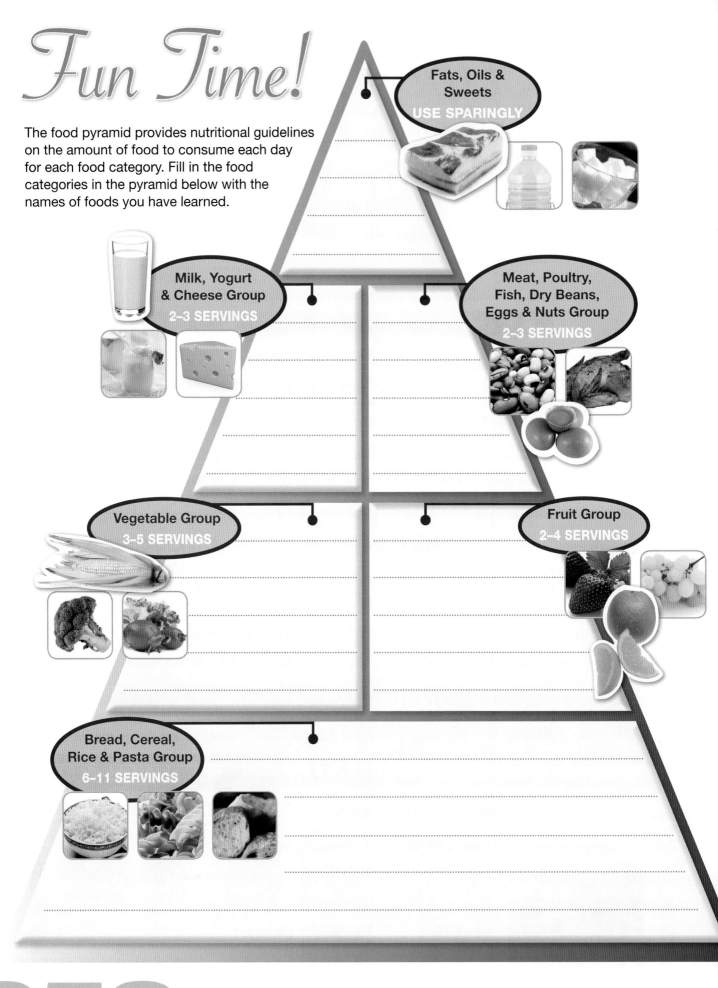

Fats, Oils & Sweets
USE SPARINGLY

Milk, Yogurt & Cheese Group
2–3 SERVINGS

Meat, Poultry, Fish, Dry Beans, Eggs & Nuts Group
2–3 SERVINGS

Vegetable Group
3–5 SERVINGS

Fruit Group
2–4 SERVINGS

Bread, Cereal, Rice & Pasta Group
6–11 SERVINGS

I have learned...

Core Vocabulary

吃 *v.*		chī	to eat	碗 *m.w.*		wǎn	*(used for dishes served in bowls)*
喝 *v.*		hē	to drink	盘 *m.w.*	盤	pán	*(used for dishes served on plates)*
好吃 *phr.*		hǎochī	tasty; delicious *(used for food)*	碟 *m.w.*		dié	*(used for dishes served on small plates)*
好喝 *phr.*		hǎohē	tasty; delicious *(used for drinks)*	份 *m.w.*		fèn	*(used for dishes that come in portions or servings)*
酸 *adj.*		suān	sour	块 *m.w.*	塊	kuài	*(mainly used for cakes and pastries)*
甜 *adj.*		tián	sweet	杯 *m.w.*		bēi	*(used for drinks served in cups)*
苦 *adj.*		kǔ	bitter	瓶 *m.w.*		píng	*(used for bottled drinks)*
辣 *adj.*		là	spicy	罐 *m.w.*		guàn	*(used for drinks in a can)*
咸 *adj.*	鹹	xián	salty	点 *v.*	點	diǎn	to order
淡 *adj.*		dàn	bland	来 *v.*	來	lái	to bring; to send
要 *v. / aux v.*		yào	to want	再 *adv.*		zài	again, another
还是 *conj.*	還是	háishì	or				

Common Food Ingredients

生菜		shēngcài	lettuce	猪肉	豬肉	zhūròu	pork
菠菜		bōcài	spinach	羊肉		yángròu	mutton
芹菜		qíncài	celery	鱼	魚	yú	fish
白菜		báicài	Chinese cabbage	虾	蝦	xiā	prawn
西兰花	西蘭花	xīlánhuā	broccoli	苹果	蘋果	píngguǒ	apple
番茄		fānqié	tomato	橙子		chéngzi	orange
玉米		yùmǐ	corn	西瓜		xīguā	watermelon
辣椒		làjiāo	chili peper	草莓		cǎoméi	strawberry
牛奶		niúnǎi	milk	葡萄		pútao	grape
黄油		huángyóu	butter	香蕉		xiāngjiāo	banana
奶酪		nǎilào	cheese	鸡蛋	雞蛋	jīdàn	egg
鸡肉	雞肉	jīròu	chicken	豆腐		dòufu	beancurd
牛肉		niúròu	beef	糖		táng	sugar

盐	鹽	yán	salt	番茄酱	番茄醬	fānqiéjiàng	ketchup
胡椒粉		hújiāofěn	pepper				

Common Chinese Foods

米饭	米飯	mǐfàn	rice	海鲜炒面	海鲜炒麵	hǎixiānchǎomiàn	seafood fried noodles
面条	麵條	miàntiáo	noodles	花生粥		huāshēngzhōu	peanut porridge
油条	油條	yóutiáo	fried dough stick	鱼粥	魚粥	yúzhōu	fish porridge
包子		bāozi	meat or vegetable bun	糖醋排骨		tángcùpáigǔ	sweet and sour pork
馒头	饅頭	mántou	bun	北京烤鸭	北京烤鴨	Běijīng kǎoyā	Peking duck
锅贴	鍋貼	guōtiē	pan-fried dumpling	中国茶	中國茶	Zhōngguóchá	Chinese tea
饺子	餃子	jiǎozi	dumpling	宫保鸡丁	宮保雞丁	gōngbǎo jīdīng	spicy chicken
春卷		chūnjuǎn	spring roll	蒸鱼	蒸魚	zhēngyú	steamed fish
馄饨汤	餛飩湯	húntuntāng	wanton soup	麻婆豆腐		mápó dòufu	spicy beancurd
酸辣汤	酸辣湯	suānlàtāng	hot and sour soup	鱼香肉丝	魚香肉絲	yúxiāng ròusī	shredded pork in spicy sauce
蛋花汤	蛋花湯	dànhuātāng	egg drop soup	豆浆	豆漿	dòujiāng	soybean milk
蛋炒饭	蛋炒飯	dànchǎofàn	egg fried rice	红豆汤	紅豆湯	hóngdòutāng	red bean soup
扬州炒饭	揚州炒飯	Yángzhōuchǎofàn	Yangzhou fried rice	芝麻汤圆	芝麻湯圓	zhīma tāngyuán	dumpling with sesame filling
素炒面	素炒麵	sùchǎomiàn	vegetarian fried noodles				

Common Western Foods

面包	麵包	miànbāo	bread	果汁		guǒzhī	fruit juice
麦片	麥片	màipiàn	cereal	沙拉		shālā	salad
咸肉	鹹肉	xiánròu	bacon	番茄汤	番茄湯	fānqiétāng	tomato soup
火腿		huǒtuǐ	ham	热狗	熱狗	règǒu	hotdog
香肠	香腸	xiāngcháng	sausage	汉堡	漢堡	hànbǎo	burger
炒蛋		chǎodàn	scrambled eggs	披萨	披薩	pīsà	pizza
烘豆		hōngdòu	baked beans	薯条	薯條	shǔtiáo	French fries
果酱	果醬	guǒjiàng	jam	牛排		niúpái	steak
咖啡		kāfēi	coffee	鸡排	雞排	jīpái	chicken fillet
茶		chá	tea	猪排	豬排	zhūpái	pork chop

羊排		yángpái	lamb chop	可乐	可樂	kělè	coke
意大利面	意大利麵	yìdàlìmiàn	spaghetti	蛋糕		dàngāo	cake
三明治		sānmíngzhì	sandwich	冰淇淋		bīngqílín	ice cream

SENTENCE PATTERNS

你吃什么？我吃饺子。

你喝什么？我喝中国茶。

汉堡好吃吗？汉堡很好吃。

可乐好喝吗？可乐很好喝。

葡萄很酸。西瓜很甜。咖啡很苦。汤很辣。培根很咸。粥很淡。

我喜欢吃饺子，也喜欢吃热狗。

我最喜欢吃鱼。我最不喜欢吃沙拉。

你要(吃)什么？我要(吃)炒饭。

你要(喝)什么？我要(喝)果汁。

你喜欢吃炒饭还是炒面。

你喜欢喝什么？咖啡还是茶。

碗、碟、盘、份、杯、块、片、个

你要点什么菜？来两个包子，再来一碗面。

I can do!

Interpretive Communication

❑ I can understand when someone asks if I want a certain food.

❑ I can read the names of fruits and vegetables in Chinese.

❑ I can understand when someone tells me his or her food and drink preferences.

❑ I can understand yes-no questions on foods and drinks.

❑ I can read and understand a simple menu.

Interpersonal Communication

❑ I can ask and answer questions about food I like and dislike.

❑ I can share information about the tastes of the foods I eat.

❑ I can ask and answer choice-type questions about food and drink.

❑ I can exchange information on likes and dislikes as well as food and drink preferences, including stating the degree of preference.

Presentational Communication

❑ I can describe the tastes of foods in general and in detail.

❑ I can create a menu of foods I would like to eat.

❑ I can write a simple grocery shopping list.

❑ I can tell others about the foods I like and dislike.

❑ I can order and specify a Chinese dish.

❑ I can order a beverage.

❑ I can write the words for some Chinese food items.

❑ I can state what I want and don't want to eat.

Cultural Knowledge

❑ I can name some fruits that are grown in China.

❑ I can name some popular Chinese dishes and beverages.

❑ I can talk about the growing trend of eating fast-foods in China.

❑ I can talk about the history of chopsticks.

❑ I can talk about food symbolism in Chinese culture.

❑ I can tell the order of courses in a Chinese meal.

APPENDICES

267

APPENDICES · 附录

后年 n.		hòunián	the year after next	100
后天 n.		hòutiān	the day after tomorrow	104
胡椒粉 n.		hújiāofěn	pepper	238
花生粥 n.		huāshēngzhōu	peanut porridge	239
滑雪 v.		huá xuě	to ski	218
画画 v.	畫畫	huàhuà	to draw	220
画家 n.	畫家	huàjiā	artist	226
化学 n.	化學	huàxué	chemistry	181
黄色 n.	黃色	huángsè	yellow	178
黄油 n.	黃油	huángyóu	butter	238
会 aux.v.	會	huì	can; be able to	222
馄饨汤 n.	餛飩湯	húntuntāng	wanton soup	239
火腿 n.		huǒtuǐ	ham	240

J

鸡 n.	鷄	jī	chicken	150
鸡蛋 n.	鷄蛋	jīdàn	egg	238
鸡排	鷄排	jīpái	chicken fillet	240
鸡肉	鷄肉	jīròu	chicken	238
几 num.	幾	jǐ	how many	85
记者 n.	記者	jìzhě	journalist	226
家¹ n.		jiā	home	58
家² n.		jiā	home; family	133
肩膀 n.		jiānbǎng	shoulder	139
健康 n.		jiànkāng	good health	118
将来 n.	將來	jiānglái	in the future	226
饺子 n.	餃子	jiǎozi	dumpling	239
脚 n.	腳	jiǎo	foot	139
叫 v.		jiào	call; be called	28
教师 n.	教師	jiàoshī	teacher	226
教室 n.		jiàoshì	classroom	170
教学楼 n.	教學樓	jiàoxuélóu	school building	170
节 m.w.	節	jié	(used for class periods)	196
节日 n.	節日	jiérì	holiday; festival	118
姐姐 n.	姊姊	jiějie / zǐzi	older sister	128
借 v.		jiè	to lend; to borrow	180
今年 n.		jīnnián	this year	100
今天 n.		jīntiān	today	84

近 adj.		jìn	near	174
警察 n.		jǐngchá	policeman	226
九 num.		jiǔ	nine	72
舅舅 n.		jiùjiu	uncle, mother's brother	131

K

咖啡 n.		kāfēi	coffee	240
看电视 phr.	看電視	kàn diànshì	to watch TV	203
看电影 phr.	看電影	kàn diànyǐng	to watch a movie	203
看书 v.	看書	kànshū	to read	220
科学家 n.	科學家	kēxuéjiā	scientist	226
可乐 n.	可樂	kělè	coke	240
刻 n.		kè	quarter of an hour	89
课 n.	課	kè	lesson; class; course	183
课 n.	課	kè	class period	196
客厅 n.	客廳	kètīng	living room	206
口 m.w.		kǒu	(used for members in the family)	133
苦 adj.		kǔ	bitter	245
块 m.w.	塊	kuài	(used for something cubical or flat in shape)	178
块 m.w.	塊	kuài	(mainly used for cakes and pastries)	252
快 adj.		kuài	fast	224
快乐 adj.	快樂	kuàilè	happy; joyful	118

L

辣 adj.		là	spicy	245
辣椒 n.		làjiāo	chili pepper	238
来 v.	來	lái	to bring; send	254
篮球 n.	籃球	lánqiú	basketball	218
蓝色 n.	籃色	lánsè	blue	178
老虎 n.		lǎohǔ	tiger	152
老师 n.	老師	lǎoshī	teacher	24
了 part.		le	(used at the end of a sentence to indicate that something has taken place)	208
累 adj.		lèi	tired	34
离 prep.	離	lí	(in giving distances) from	174
李 n.		Lǐ	(a common Chinese surname)	26
里(边) prep.	裏(邊)	lǐ(bian)	inside	171
历史 n.	歷史	lìshǐ	history	181
零 num.		líng	zero	72

六 num.		liù	six	72
龙 n.	龍	lóng	dragon	161
绿色 n.	綠色	lǜsè	green	178
律师 n.	律師	lǜshī	lawyer	226

M

妈妈 n.	媽媽	māma	mother	26
麻婆豆腐 n.		mápó dòufu	spicy beancurd	239
马 n.	馬	mǎ	horse	150
吗 part.	嗎	ma	(a question word)	32
麦片 n.	麥片	màipiàn	cereal	240
馒头 n.	饅頭	mántou	bun	239
慢 adj.		màn	slow	224
忙 adj.		máng	busy	34
猫 n.	貓	māo	cat	150
眉毛 n.		méimao	eyebrow	139
没有 v.	沒有	méiyou	do not have	137
每 adv.		měi	every	228
美国 n.	美國	Měiguó	U.S.A.	49
美国人 n.	美國人	Měiguórén	American	50
美术 n.	美術	měishù	art	181
妹妹 n.		mèimei	younger sister	128
门 n.	門	mén	door	176
门 m.w.	門	mén	(used for lesson/class/course)	183
米饭 n.	米飯	mǐfàn	rice	239
面包 n.	麵包	miànbāo	bread	240
面条 n.	麵條	miàntiáo	noodles	239
秒 n.		miǎo	second of a minute	87
名 m.w.		míng	(used for position in a competition)	81
名字 n.		míngzi	name	37
明年 n.		míngnián	next year	100
明天 n.		míngtiān	tomorrow	84
墨西哥 n.		Mòxīgē	Mexico	49
母亲 n.	母親	mǔqīn	mother	128

N

哪 pron.		nǎ	where; which	50
哪里 pron.	哪裏	nǎlǐ	where	56

哪儿 pron.	哪兒	nǎr	where	58
那儿 pron.	那兒	nàr	there	58
奶酪 n.		nǎilào	cheese	238
奶奶 n.		nǎinai	paternal grandmother	131
南 n.		nán	south	60
南非 n.		Nánfēi	South Africa	49
男 n.		nán	male	50
男孩 n.		nánhái	boy	136
呢 part.		ne	(used to form questions)	117
你 pron.		nǐ	you (singular)	22
你好 phr.		nǐ hǎo	hello	22
你早 phr.		nǐ zǎo	good morning	23
你们 pron.	你們	nǐmen	you (plural)	24
年 n.		nián	year	100
年纪 n.	年紀	niánjì	age	113
鸟 n.	鳥	niǎo	bird	150
您 pron.		nín	you (singular; the polite form)	22
牛 n.		niú	cow, ox	150
牛奶 n.		niúnǎi	milk	238
牛排 n.		niúpái	steak	240
牛肉 n.		niúròu	beef	238
女 n.		nǚ	female	50
女孩 n.		nǚhái	girl	136

P

爬 v.		pá	crawl, climb	160
盘 m.w.	盤	pán	(used for dishes served on plates)	252
旁边 n.	旁邊	pángbiān	beside	172
胖 adj.		pàng	fat	140
跑 v.		pǎo	run	160
跑步 v.		pǎobù	to jog	218
披萨 n.	披薩	pīsà	pizza	240
匹 m.w.		pǐ	(used mainly for horses)	157
乒乓球 n.		pīngpāngqiú	table tennis	218
瓶 m.w.		píng	(used for bottled drinks)	252
苹果 n.	蘋果	píngguǒ	apple	238
葡萄 n.		pútao	grape	238

Q

七 num.		qī	seven	72
起床 phr.		qǐchuáng	to get out of bed	203
千 num.		qiān	thousand	78
铅笔 n.	鉛筆	qiānbǐ	pencil	178
前(边) n.	前邊	qián(bian)	in the front	172
前年 n.		qiánnián	the year before last	100
前天 n.		qiántiān	the day before yesterday	104
墙 n.		qiáng	wall	176
芹菜 n.		qíncài	celery	238
去年 n.		qùnián	last year	100

R

热狗 n.	熱狗	règǒu	hotdog	240
人 n.		rén	person, people	50
日 n.		rì	day; date (written Chinese)	104
日本 n.		Rìběn	Japan	49

S

三 num.		sān	three	72
三明治 n.		sānmíngzhì	sandwich	240
沙拉 n.		shālā	salad	240
上 prep.		shàng	up; above	82
上个星期 phr.	上個星期	shàng gè xīngqī	last week	108
上个月 phr.	上個月	shàng gè yuè	last month	108
上海 n.		Shànghǎi	Shanghai	56
上课 phr.	上課	shàngkè	to attend class; class starts	197
上网 phr.	上網	shàngwǎng	to go on the Internet	208
(上网)聊天 phr.	(上網)聊天	(shàngwǎng) liáotiān	to chat online	208
上午 n.		shàngwǔ	morning	82
上学 phr.	上學	shàngxué	to attend school	197
蛇 n.		shé	snake	152
谁 pron.	誰	shéi, shuí	who	30
身体 n.	身體	shēntǐ	body; health	118
什么 pron.	甚麼	shénme	what	37
生菜 n.		shēngcài	lettuce	238
生日 n.		shēngrì	birthday	115
生物 n.		shēngwù	biology	181

狮子 n.	獅子	shīzi	lion	152
十 num.		shí	ten	72
是 v.		shì	am, is, are (verb "to be")	28
手 n.		shǒu	hand	139
瘦 adj.		shòu	slim	140
书 n.	書	shū	book	176
书包 n.	書包	shūbāo	bag	178
书房 n.	書房	shūfáng	study room	206
叔叔 n.		shūshu	uncle	26
叔叔 n.		shūshu	uncle, father's younger brother	131
属 v.	屬	shǔ	be born in the year of	164
鼠 n.		shǔ	rat	164
薯条 n.	薯條	shǔtiáo	French fries	240
数学 n.	數學	shùxué	mathematics	181
刷牙 phr.		shuāyá	to brush one's teeth	203
睡觉 phr.	睡覺	shuìjiào	to go to bed; to sleep	203
四 num.		sì	four	72
素炒面 n.	素炒麵	sùchǎomiàn	vegetarian fried noodles	239
酸 adj.		suān	sour	245
酸辣汤 n.	酸辣湯	suānlàtāng	hot and sour soup	239
岁 n.	歲	suì	year of age	113

T

他 pron.		tā	he; him	28
她 pron.		tā	she; her	28
它 pron.		tā	it	150
太极拳 n.	太極拳	tàijíquán	Taiji	218
弹钢琴 phr.	彈鋼琴	tán gāngqín	to play piano	220
糖 n.		táng	sugar	238
糖醋排骨 n.		tángcùpáigǔ	sweet and sour pork	239
踢 v.		tī	to kick	218
体育 n.	體育	tǐyù	physical education	181
体育馆 n.	體育館	tǐyùguǎn	gymnasium	170
天 n.		tiān	day	81
天天 phr.		tiāntiān	every day	228
甜 adj.		tián	sweet	245
条 m.w.	條	tiáo	(used mainly for animals with long bodies)	157
跳 v.		tiào	jump	160

271

你好！/ 您好！   45

你们好！/ 同学们好！

老师，您好！/ 爸爸，您好！/ 妈妈，您好！

王叔叔、李阿姨，你们好！

再见！

我是小伟。她是芳芳。他是马丁。

你是谁？我是芳芳。

你好吗？我很好，谢谢！/ 还可以。

你忙吗？我很忙。/ 我不忙。

你叫什么名字？/ 你叫什么？

我叫李小成。

你姓什么？我姓王。

您贵姓？我姓张。

你是哪国人？我是美国人。   67

你是中国人吗？对，我是中国人。/
不是，我是英国人。

她也是美国人吗？对，我们都是美国人。

你是哪里人？我是北京人。

你家在哪儿？我家在这儿。

你住哪儿？我住东边。

现在几点？   96

现在七点。

现在六点二十五分。

现在三点三刻。

现在八点半。

现在差一刻四点。

今年是2011年。   124

上个月是四月。

今天二月五号。

明天星期六。

下个星期五是七号。

三年；七天

两个月；四个星期

你多大？/ 你几岁？

我的生日是一月三号。

你呢？/ 你的呢？

祝你生日快乐！

这是谁？这是我父亲。   146

那是谁？那是我母亲。

这是你爸爸吗？对，这是我爸爸。

那是你妈妈吗？不是，那是我阿姨。

你家有几口人？我家有三口人。

爸爸、妈妈和我

一个男孩，两个女孩

你有哥哥吗？有。我有一个哥哥。

你有没有姐姐？我没有姐姐。

我的头发。我的耳朵。

我姐姐很高。

我弟弟很胖。

这是什么动物？这是狗。   166

动物园有熊猫，还有狮子。

你喜欢不喜欢小狗？我喜欢小狗。

我喜欢小狗，也喜欢小猫。

我最不喜欢蛇。

一只小狗、一条蛇、六头猪、两匹马

你家有狗吗？有，我家有一只狗。

你家有没有猫？没有，我家没有猫。

小鸟飞、小鱼游、小狗跑、乌龟爬、兔子跳

学校里有什么？学校里有教学楼，　　　190
有图书馆，还有体育馆。

教学楼外有什么？教学楼外有操场。

你家离学校远吗？我家离学校很远。

教室离图书馆近吗？教室离图书馆很近。

教室里有什么？教室里有黑板、桌子和椅子。

墙上有什么？墙上有白板和钟。

借我一支笔，行吗？行，给你。

你有什么课？

你有几门课？我有八门课。

你学过生物吗？我学过生物。你学过化学吗？
我没学过化学。

你今天有什么课？我今天有英语课。　　　214

星期一你有什么课？星期一我有中文课。

你今天有几节课？我今天有六节课。

你今天几点上课？几点下课？
我今天早上八点上课，九点下课。

你今天几点上学？几点放学？我今天上午
八点上学，下午三点放学。

现在十点。

十点以前是什么课？十点以前是英语课。

十点以后是什么课？十点以后是数学课。

明天从九点到十点你有什么课？我有中文课。

你几点起床？我早上七点半起床。

你在哪儿上课？我在教室上课。

昨天晚上你做什么了？我上网了。

你有什么爱好？我喜欢游泳。　　　234

你的爱好是什么？我的爱好是唱歌。

你会打网球吗？我会打网球。我不会打网球。

他会不会打太极拳？会／不会。

他打篮球打得好吗？他打篮球打得很好／
打得不好。

她游泳游得怎么样？她游得很快。／
她游得很慢。

你想当什么？我想当运动员。

我天天打网球。我每个星期二和星期四
踢足球。

你吃什么？我吃饺子。　　　261

你喝什么？我喝中国茶。

汉堡好吃吗？汉堡很好吃。

可乐好喝吗？可乐很好喝。

葡萄很酸。西瓜很甜。咖啡很苦。汤很辣。
培根很咸。粥很淡。

我喜欢吃饺子，也喜欢吃热狗。

我最喜欢吃鱼。我最不喜欢吃沙拉。

你要(吃)什么？我要(吃)炒饭。

你要(喝)什么？我要(喝)果汁。

你喜欢吃炒饭还是炒面。

你喜欢喝什么？咖啡还是茶。

碗、碟、盘、份、杯、块、片、个

你要点什么菜？来两个包子，再来一碗面。